W9-BSD-157

Target ISRAEL

TIM LAHAYE
AND
ED HINDSON

HARVEST HOUSE PUBLISHERS
EUGENE, OREGON

TARGET ISRAEL
Copyright © 2015 Tim LaHaye Ministries and Ed Hindson
Published by Harvest House Publishers
Eugene, Oregon 97402
www.harvesthousepublishers.com

Library of Congress Cataloging-in-Publication Data
    LaHaye, Tim F.
    Target Israel / Tim LaHaye and Ed Hindson.
        pages cm
    ISBN 978-0-7369-6449-4 (pbk.)
    ISBN 978-0-7369-6450-0 (eBook)
    1. Bible—Prophecies—Israel. I. Title.
    BS649.P3L35 2015
    220.1'5—dc23

                                                                    2014048837

Printed in the United States of America

        15 16 17 18 19 20 21 22 23 / VP-JH / 10 9 8 7 6 5 4 3 2 1

To my faithful wife of 68 years and best friend, Beverly,
and our four children: Linda, Larry, Lee, and Lori,
and their spouses Murf, Sharron, and Greg.
—Tim

To my incredible wife of 48 years, Donna,
and our children: Linda, Christy, and Jon,
and their spouses Andy, Jeff, and Amanda.
—Ed

We are both thrilled that we have no greater joy
than to know that our children are "walking in truth"
(2 John 4).

*It shall happen in that day that I will make Jerusalem
a very heavy stone for all peoples; all who would heave it away
will surely be cut to pieces, though all nations of the earth
are gathered against it.*

Zechariah 12:3

Contents

A New and Growing Crisis

Though we are both Gentiles by birth and followers of Jesus Christ, we have long loved the Jewish people and the nation of Israel. That's how it should be with every believer. Scripture and history offer at least three important reasons for Christians to care for the Jewish people and their land.

First, the founder of our faith, Jesus Christ, was Jewish. He was miraculously conceived in the womb of the Jewish virgin Mary. He was raised the son of a Jewish father named Joseph in the Jewish city of Nazareth. Though betrayed by His own people into the hands of Roman authorities, His death on the cross led to His resurrection on the third day in Jerusalem, the capital city of Israel. The church soon began in this same Jewish capital on the Day of Pentecost (Acts 2), growing rapidly among Jews before expanding to Gentiles across the world.

Second, the Bible's human authors were almost exclusively Jewish people. From Moses, the author of Genesis, to the apostle John, the author of Revelation, the books of the Bible are the result of

Jewish writers who were guided by the Holy Spirit to produce the words that guide our Christian faith today. With the possible exception of Luke, who authored the Gospel of Luke and Acts, every book of the Bible was authored by a Jewish writer. In fact, many scholars believe Luke was Jewish. He was led to faith in Christ by the Jewish apostle Paul.

Third, the Jewish people founded the church in Jerusalem. Without the leadership of the Jewish apostles of Jesus and the courageous early followers of Christ, the church we enjoy today would not be what it is. These early Jewish Christians risked their lives for the gospel and many were martyred for their faith in Christ.

The history of the United States has also been greatly influenced by its relationship with the nation of Israel and the Jewish people. Many of America's great leaders have recognized God's covenant to Abraham in Genesis 12:3: "I will bless those who bless you, and I will curse him who curses you; and in you all the families of the earth shall be blessed." When Israel once again became a nation in 1948, the United States played a major role in supporting its recognition among the international community. America's efforts in World War II also affirmed its support of the Jewish people, saving many lives from Jewish concentration camps and from the wrath of Adolf Hitler's Nazi Germany.

Today, America faces a new and growing crisis with regard to its historic relationship with Israel. The Jewish nation is surrounded by many hostile neighbors who both fail to recognize its existence and vow to wipe it off the map. Further, many of these neighbors are growing an alliance of nations that stand opposed to Israel and its sovereignty. Amidst these rising tensions, Western nations increasingly speak of peace, yet show little action to support Israel. These "inactions" leave the Jewish people in a vulnerable position that ultimately shows the protection of a loving God who watches over the nation's borders.

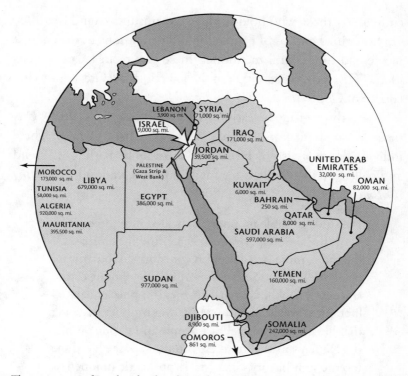

The tiny nation of Israel and its hostile Muslim neighbors. The Arab nations total more than 5,000,000 square miles, whereas Israel is only 9,000 square miles. Excerpted from Randall Price, *Fast Facts on the Middle East Conflict* (Eugene, OR: Harvest House, 2003), p. 82. Used with permission.

In this book, we'll look at the biblical information that reveals Israel as God's super sign of the end times. Unfortunately, a growing number of Christians do not interpret the Bible literally with regard to Israel. Instead, Christian leaders and movements popularly advocate the erroneous teachings of what is known as Replacement Theology. The proponents of this view believe that the church has replaced Israel in God's plan for the future. Instead of looking ahead to God's future blessings upon Israel, those who hold to Replacement Theology want to claim God's blessings upon the church. Yet those who hold to this view misunderstand the three God-ordained groups of people the Bible mentions in the context of the end times. Paul mentioned these groups in 1 Corinthians 10:32: "Give no offense, either to the Jews or to the Greeks or to the church of God."

These three groups clearly include Gentiles, Jews, and Christians. What about Jews who have accepted Christ by faith? These individuals are Jewish by birth and Christian by faith. Our friend and colleague Dr. Thomas Ice made this observation in *Charting the End Times*:

> The study of Bible prophecy is divided into three major areas: the nations (Gentiles), Israel, and the church. Of the three, more detail is given concerning God's future plans for His nation Israel than for the nations or the church. When the church takes these prophecies to Israel literally, as we do, then we see a great prophetic agenda that lies ahead for Israel as a people and nation. When the church spiritualizes these promises, as she has done too often in history, then Israel's prophetic uniqueness is subsumed and merged unrealistically into the church. But if we handle Scripture carefully, we can see that God has an amazing and blessed future planned for individual Jews and national Israel. That's why we believe Israel is God's "super sign" of the end times.
>
> God's promises to Abraham and Israel are unconditional and guaranteed through the various subsequent covenants. A definite pattern for Israel's future history was prophesied in Deuteronomy before the Jews set even one foot in the Promised Land (Deuteronomy 4:28-31). The predicted pattern for God's program with Israel was to be as follows: They would enter the land under Joshua, and they would eventually turn away from the Lord and be expelled from the land and scattered among the

Gentile nations. From there the Lord would regather the Jewish people during the latter days and they would pass through the Tribulation. Toward the end of the Tribulation they would recognize their Messiah and be regenerated. Christ would then return to Earth and rescue Israel from the nations who are gathered at Armageddon to exterminate the Jews. A second regathering of the nation would then occur in preparation for the millennial reign with Christ, during which time all of Israel's unfulfilled promises will be realized. This pattern is developed by the prophets and reinforced in the New Testament.

As with the church and the nations, God is moving His chosen people—Israel—into place for the future fulfillment of His prophecies relating to the nation. He has already brought the Jewish people back to their ancient land (1948) and has given them Jerusalem (1967). However, the current situation in Israel is one of constant turmoil and crisis, especially in the old city of Jerusalem. Eventually Israel will sign a covenant with the Antichrist, and that will initiate the seven-year Tribulation.

Israel's regathering and the turmoil are specific signs that God's end-time program is on the verge of springing into full gear. In addition, the fact that all three streams of prophecy (the nations, Israel, and the church) are converging for the first time in history constitutes a sign in itself. This is why many students of prophecy believe that we are near the last days. If you want to know where history is headed, simply keep your eye on what God is doing with Israel.[1]

The gospel of Jesus Christ is for all ethnic groups: Asians, Africans, Europeans, Jews, Arabs—no one is excluded. God is not anti-Arab, and neither are we. He loves the Arab people as He does all people. Twice, He could have solved the so-called Arab-Israeli conflict 4000 years ago by letting Ishmael, father of the Arabs, die in the desert (Genesis 16:7-11; 21:17-18). Instead, the Lord Himself intervened to spare Ishmael's life and promised to make him a great nation, and indeed He has.

The real conflict in the Middle East is more *religious* than ethnic. Islam is a religion, whereas Arab is an ethnicity. Not all Arabs are Muslims. There are many Christian Arabs who are politically and socially caught behind the "Islamic Curtain." They need our constant prayers, help, and support. Also, many Muslims are not Arabs. For example, there are Turks, Kurds, Afghans, Iranians, and Indonesians who are not ethnic Arabs. So the real threat to Israel and the West is religious fanaticism.

In this book, our goal is to help you better understand the biblical importance of Israel. God's hand of blessing has been upon the Jewish people all through their history—from the beginning with Abraham and Sarah, during the escape from Egyptian slavery under the leadership of Moses, and during numerous other events found both in the Bible and throughout history. For centuries the Jewish people have been scattered around the world, but in recent decades God has regathered them into the modern-day nation of Israel. As for the future, the Bible speaks of both times of judgment and blessing upon Israel, culminating in a new heavens and earth that will include a heavenly city called the New Jerusalem.

One of the key sources of hatred against Israel these days is *extremist* Islamic factions which are determined to reconquer any land once held by Islamic forces. This includes the modern nation of Israel. Not all Muslims are extremists, but unfortunately those who are number well into the thousands and are thoroughly committed to the destruction and elimination of Israel. These radical terrorists have believed the lies of Satan that blaspheme the nature of God and His commands to live holy lives according to the Bible, and they offer a profane and immoral eternity to those who give their life to advance Muslim dominance over the entire world.

CHAPTER 1

Israel in the Crossfire

Israel has been the target of Islamic extremists since its miraculous rebirth as a nation in 1948. Now, more than 65 years later, she is still under constant attack. Israel exists today on much of the biblical Promised Land despite facing continual threats from Islamic extremists on nearly every border. She has had to endure suicide and homicide bombers, rocket and missile attacks, genocidal threats from her Middle Eastern neighbors, and political pressure from America and Europe. Throughout the summer of 2014 Israel was bombarded by Palestinian rockets coming out of Gaza day after day despite international calls for a cease-fire. By the end of the conflict more than 2000 Palestinians and 154 Israelis had been killed in one of the worst conflicts in Israel in the last 50 years.

On August 26, 2014, the Palestinians and Israelis agreed to a ceasefire following 50 days of conflict. More than 4450 rockets had been fired into Israel from Gaza. Further, this cease-fire was the twelfth one in seven weeks. Hamas and radical Islamists in Gaza had broken the 11 previous agreements, offering only tentative hope that the latest accord would hold.

Those in Gaza, however, had little choice at this point. The land and local economy had been decimated by the strategic and specific military response of Israel. Most of Gaza's network of tunnels reaching under Israeli territory had been destroyed, as well as many missile launch locations. Yet despite this temporary agreement, the Palestinian opponents of Israel continue to refuse to recognize Israel as a nation and are still determined to eventually take the land for themselves and eliminate the Jewish people.

Hamas terrorists in Gaza are not alone in this desire. As recently as November 2014, Iran's Supreme Leader Ayatollah Ali Khamenei proposed, via Twitter, his latest plan to destroy Israel, and urged that the international community should accept his plan. He raised nine key questions regarding the why and how of implementing an effort to eliminate Israel:

1. Why should the Zionist regime be eliminated?

2. What does elimination of Israel mean in the viewpoint of Imam Khomeini?

3. What is the proper way of eliminating Israel?

4. What happened to the non-Palestinian emigrants?

5. How will the proposed referendum succeed?

6. Until a referendum is held, how should Israel be confronted?

7. What is the most urgent action to take to militarily confront Israel?

8. What solutions are not acceptable?

9. Why do we oppose compromise goals?[1]

Perhaps the most disturbing of Khamenei's answers is the one to question six. He notes, "Up until the days when this homicidal and infanticidal regime is eliminated through a referendum, powerful confrontation and resolute and armed resistance is the cure of this ruinous regime. The only means of confronting a regime which commits crimes beyond one's thought and imagination is a resolute and armed conflict." Though he warns against "a classical war by the army of Muslim countries," he certainly approves of arming the West Bank and calling its people to action against Israel.[2]

As if such hostile language were not enough, Khamenei also serves as the supreme leader of a nation that is rapidly developing its nuclear capabilities—including the technology necessary to produce nuclear weapons.

A November 24, 2014 deadline for the US government to negotiate with Iran about its nuclear capabilities came and went with no diminished impact on the nation's ongoing efforts. In fact, the pace of development shows signs of accelerating. The *New York Times* reported that Russia has recently agreed to build two new nuclear facilities in Iran, with the possibility of six additional sites to come. Olli Heinonen, a 27-year veteran of the International Atomic Energy Agency, said that Iran could have up to five times more advance centrifuges than previously admitted. Israeli prime minister Benjamin Netanyahu continues to speak out against these activities, arguing that Iran remains a greater threat than ISIS.[3]

Within Israel itself, the number of terrorist acts committed against the Jewish people continues to grow. On October 29, 2014, for example, terrorists attempted to assassinate a Jewish activist known for supporting the reconstruction of a Jewish temple on the Temple Mount. When Israeli officials briefly closed the Temple Mount the next day, Palestinian President Abbas declared the move "a declaration of war."[4]

Less than a week later, an Israeli border officer was killed and 13 civilians were wounded when an Arab man used a car in a terror attack in Jerusalem. Less than two weeks after this incident, five people were killed, including three US-Israeli citizens, in a grisly attack on a Jerusalem synagogue. The two attackers were armed with butcher knives and a gun and were later shot dead, but not before they hacked four Jewish rabbis to death.[5]

In addition to these ongoing threats from Hamas and nearby neighbors, al-Qaeda still holds a presence in the area. Hezbollah opposes Israel in the north, and a variety of other anti-Israeli terrorist factions are based in Syria, Yemen, Lebanon, and North Africa. And more recently, one terrorist organization has ascended into prominence because it is so violent. Its proponents are working to overtake the entire Middle East. They are known as ISIS.

ISIS: A Serious Threat

As if "war and rumors of war" from Gaza, Iran, and within Israel's borders were not enough, the ISIS (also known as the Islamic State) has emerged as the newest threat all across the Middle East. Despite the fact Osama bin Laden has passed from the scene and President Obama has claimed that al-Qaeda has been decimated, the battle against terrorism has not abated.

Back in 2008, with the help of US military involvement, the jihadist movement in Iraq had largely been defeated. But today, ISIS has emerged as among the most powerful terrorist groups in world history. The eye-opening book *Rise of ISIS* notes,

> ISIS is stronger than any jihadist group in world history. Americans have long—and rightly—feared al-Qaeda. After all, it carried out the most devastating attack ever on American soil. But if we have feared and fought al-Qaeda, consider the following facts about ISIS:
>
> - ISIS is more brutal than al-Qaeda, so brutal that al-Qaeda tried to persuade ISIS to change its tactics.
>
> - ISIS is the "world's richest terrorist group."
>
> - ISIS controls more firepower and territory than any jihadist organization in history. ISIS has reportedly

seized "40kg of radioactive uranium in Iraq," raising fears that it could construct a "dirty bomb" that could spread deadly radiation in the atmosphere, rendering entire areas uninhabitable and killing or sickening everyone within the radius of its radiation cloud.[6]

Shortly before ISIS's conquest of large portions of Syria and Iraq, President Obama had previously noted ISIS as a "JV team" yet later admitted intelligence reports had underestimated the strength of this militant movement.[7] Its recent activities have included:

- Slaughtering Christians and other non-Muslims across Iraq and Syria.

- Beheading American and British reporters and aid workers.

- Working to build a "global caliphate" that includes Lebanon, Jordan, and Israel.

- Creating its own currency based on gold and silver.

- Building alliances with similar movements in North Africa and the Middle East.

- Recruiting radical terrorists from Europe and North America.

- Seeking to rule by Sharia law (with only the Qur'an as its constitution).

- Vowing to attack American soil and raise its black flag over the White House.

The group's most recent "annual report" noted "it had carried out 1,083 assassinations and perpetrated 4,465 car bomb attacks in Iraq in 2013. Overall, there were almost 10,000 operations carried out by ISIS last year in Iraq alone, although it also expanded rapidly in Syria."[8] As of July 2014, the Iraqi civilian toll passed 5500 follow-ing attacks by ISIS.[9]

In response, a coalition of nations led by the US initiated air attacks on key ISIS strongholds in Syria and Iraq. The airstrikes had little effect, with ISIS control creeping closer to Turkey and other borders. Its leader, Abu Bakr al-Baghdadi, is claimed to hold an earned doctorate in Islamic Studies from a school in Baghdad. His movement began north of the Iraqi capital before joining with al-Qaeda in Iraq. Upon creating the Islamic State, he adopted the name Al-Khalifah Ibrahim. He was detained in an American-run prison at Camp Bucca in South Iraq for four years until 2009 before leading his current militant efforts.[10]

The strength and numbers of this terrorist faction have surged. As of August 2014, experts noted, the ISIS fighting force stands at "around 10,000, a far cry from some estimates that have placed that number as high as 80,000." Its revenue stands between one and two million US dollars *per day*. Its financial value is unknown, but at the time of this writing, the group controls numerous weapons and more than 90,000 square kilometers of land (55,923 miles).[11]

In July 2014, Christians took offense at the ISIS bombings of the traditional tombs of biblical prophets Jonah and Daniel in Mosul, Iraq. According to eyewitnesses, ISIS soldiers took "a full hour to rig the shrine with explosives before setting it [Jonah's tomb] ablaze. The shrine has reportedly been turned to dust."[12]

ISIS's YouTube videos featuring the beheadings of hostages have also captured the attention and outrage of global media. James Foley was the first American to die by beheading on August 19, 2014. He was a freelance journalist taken hostage in November 2012. Fol-lowing his brutal murder, widespread outcry came from America and the international community, leading to a more serious con-sideration of this terrorist group's activities. Despite this outcry, the beheadings continued, and, as of this writing, at least ten Kurds, three Americans, and two British aid workers have been beheaded, with several of those posted publicly online.

The persecution of Christians has also intensified in the wake of ISIS terrorist attacks across Iraq and Syria. Despite such activities, the Western church has largely failed to wake up and respond. Journalist Kirsten Powers writes, "Christians in the Middle East and Africa are being slaughtered, tortured, raped, kidnapped, beheaded, and forced to flee the birthplace of Christianity. One would think this horror might be consuming the pulpits and pews of American churches. Not so. The silence has been nearly deafening."

Kirsten further notes, "In January, Rep. Frank Wolf (R-VA) penned a letter to 300 Catholic and Protestant leaders complaining about their lack of engagement. 'Can you, as a leader in the church, help?'"[13] Though some Christians, churches, and ministries have responded to the current crisis, many have failed to move to action.

How should the US and other nations respond to ISIS? Opinions vary widely, but one popular observation came from retired three-star general and former Deputy Undersecretary of Defense for Intelligence Jerry Boykin, who believes a serious military response is necessary if we want to stop the efforts of the Islamic State. He shares:

> I have hesitated to write this posting because I have been trying to find an alternative to what I will propose here.
>
> The situation with ISIS is very serious now as I am sure that everyone is aware…So what do we need to do now? I hate to recommend this but I have considered the alternatives and I find none acceptable.[14]

Boykin then lists his recommendations, which include increasing intelligence efforts against ISIS, assigning more Special Operations teams on the ground where needed, searching out ISIS fighters with the help of antitank systems and attack helicopters, arming the

Kurds (directly rather than through Iraq's government), and stopping foreign aid or sales of arms and equipment to nations that will not help in the fight against ISIS.

While Boykin's advice may seem extreme to some, his concern is to stop the terrorists now before they become a more serious global threat. From a purely military standpoint, he is correct about the need for a firm stance. In the meantime, we need to pray for Christians in the Middle East who are being threatened and killed by members of ISIS and other extremist groups.

As ISIS continues its violent rampage across the Middle East, many Christians are asking whether this signals yet another step forward in the fulfillment of end-time prophecies. Second Timothy 3:1 does warn "that in the last days perilous times will come." We appear to be living in just such days!

In the chapters that follow, we'll look at the Bible's predictions regarding the nations that will align against Israel in the last days. As we'll discover, many will rise up against Israel, yet God will supernaturally protect the nation from harm. As Genesis 12:3 promises, God will bless those who bless Israel and curse those who curse Israel. This promise finds great significance today as we look at the increasingly strained relationship between America and Israel.

America's Cooling Relationship with Israel

The United States has long served as Israel's greatest ally in the world community. Since the founding of modern Israel in 1948, no other nation has offered as much support. Yet in recent years, there has been a shift in this historic alliance. Some have even gone so far as to describe current US-Israeli relations as a "train wreck."[15]

After a senior White House official used a vulgar reference against Israeli prime minister Benjamin Netanyahu in October 2014, *The Atlantic* declared, "The crisis in U.S.-Israel relations is officially here." In response, Netanyahu addressed the Knesset, saying, "I was personally attacked purely because I defend Israel, and despite all the attacks against me, I will continue to defend our country, I will continue to defend the citizens of Israel."[16]

Author Joel Rosenberg notes,

> It is painful to watch personal tensions growing between the White House and the State Department and the Netanyahu government at a moment when Iran's nuclear threat requires unity between two long-standing allies…Why do we see such intense emotion from the Obama team about Netanyahu, a faithful ally of the US, but never against Putin or Khamenei?[17]

Rosenberg further notes this action coincides with the biblical prediction found in Zechariah 12:2-3:

> Behold, I will make Jerusalem a cup of drunkenness to all the surrounding peoples, when they lay siege against Judah and Jerusalem. And it shall happen in that day that I will make Jerusalem a very heavy stone for all peoples; all who would heave it away will surely be cut in pieces, though all nations of the earth are gathered against it.

America's "cooling off" to Israel may be part of the fulfillment of this very passage.

Given God's promise to Israel in Genesis 12:3, we can conclude that America's future is closely connected to the kind of relation it has with Israel. Over the decades that America has stood as Israel's ally, the nation has been blessed. Yet we also have to acknowledge that when the US fails to show support for Israel, then God's blessings will be removed. Not only does Israel need America, but America also needs Israel.

Beyond America

The increasingly negative direction of America's relationship with Israel has been of concern to those who support the Jewish nation. Yet that concern has been overshadowed by the even more vocal anti-Israeli opposition expressed by various world powers in the United Nations. As author Jay Sekulow explains in his book *The Rise of ISIS*, the UN has made its anti-Israel sentiments known in a number of ways. For example, during the 2014 conflict between Hamas and Israel, the UN refused to denounce Hamas's practice of using human shields in danger zones and blamed Israel when Palestinian civilians died. And when UN officials discovered Hamas rockets hidden in UN facilities such as schools, the rockets were handed back to Hamas rather than confiscated.

Sekulow further observes:

> And lest you think this campaign to demonize and restrict Israel applies only to our closest Middle East ally and friend, and not to American forces, think again. By attacking Israel, the U.N. and the international left are trying to establish an entirely new "law of war" that would be used to try to tie America's hands as it fights terror at home and abroad. These new rules and regulations would be used to brand our own soldiers as war criminals. After all, when it comes to our own military tactics in the war against jihadist terrorists, our own military is far less restrained than Israel's.[18]

Traditionally, the anti-Israeli sentiments from the UN have had their origin from non-Western nations. However, this is changing. This is evident when one observes the source nations from which ISIS fighters originate. *Business Insider* reported,

> U.S. and European security services estimate that more than 1,000 of jihadist militants fighting in Iraq and Syria were drawn to the conflict from Western nations with some estimates putting the number as high as 3,000…700 recruits from France, 400 from the U.K., 320 from Germany, 250 from Belgium, 200 from Australia, 130 from the Netherlands, 100 from Canada, 100 from the U.S., and 51 from Spain.[19]

In fact, Western anti-Semitism has reached alarming levels. A November 2014 report noted:

> Violent anti-Semitic incidents flared up across Europe during Israel's military operation in Gaza over the summer, and ADL's recent Global 100 Survey found that anti-Semitic attitudes are still deeply entrenched on the continent, with 24 percent of the adult population in Western Europe and 34 percent in Eastern Europe holding deep-seated anti-Jewish views. [20]

Today, anti-Semitism is often masked as legitimate criticism of Israel's political and military actions. Suzanne Fields calls it the "Israelization of anti-Semitism," in which criticism of Israel is worn as a cloak to disguise Jew hatred. Pro-Palestinian demonstrations openly cry, "Death to the Jews," yet virtually no one is protesting the Syrian government which has massacred over 160,000 civilians including 1,800 Palestinians. She suggests the "Israelization" of Jew hatred has converted the nineteenth-century "Jewish question" into the twenty-first century "Israeli question." [21]

One European study that surveyed 6000 self-identified Jews noted:

- Two-thirds of respondents said that anti-Semitism was a serious problem in their country; three out of four felt it had worsened in the past five years.

- Close to a quarter said they sometimes refrained from visiting Jewish events or sites out of safety concerns. Nearly two out of five usually avoided public displays of Jewish identity such as wearing a Star of David.

- Almost one in three had considered emigrating because they did not feel safe as Jews. [22]

A July 2014 *Newsweek* magazine cover was provocatively titled,

"Exodus: Why Europe's Jews Are Fleeing Once Again." The cover article observed:

> France has suffered the worst violence, but anti-Semitism is spiking across Europe, fuelled by the war in Gaza. In Britain, the Community Security Trust (CST) says there were around 100 anti-Semitic incidents in July, double the usual number. The CST has issued a security alert for Jewish institutions. In Berlin a crowd of anti-Israel protesters had to be prevented from attacking a synagogue. In Liege, Belgium, a café owner put up a sign saying dogs were welcome, but Jews were not allowed.

> Yet for many French and European Jews, the violence comes as no surprise. Seventy years after the Holocaust, from Amiens to Athens, the world's oldest hatred flourishes anew. For some, opposition to Israeli policies is now a justification for open hatred of Jews—even though many Jews are strongly opposed to Israel's rightward lurch, and support the establishment of a Palestinian state.[23]

Facing Attack Every Day

In the years since the tragic attacks of 9/11 that took the lives of nearly 3000 people, America has faced sporadic threats to freedom. These threats are growing more common, but for the most part, they come from the other side of an ocean and aren't constant. By contrast, the people of Israel face life-and-death situations all around them every day.

Though the world cried "Never again" following the genocidal atrocities that targeted the Jewish people during World War II, today, there are a growing number of enemies working together toward the same effort—the destruction of Israel and the Jewish people.

In the pages that follow, we'll look at the biblical touch-points relevant to this targeting of Israel and offer hope regarding God's plans for today—and the future. The end continues to draw nearer, providing heightened anticipation for those who expect the return of Jesus Christ, yet causing unprecedented concern as the world spirals more and more out of control.

CHAPTER 2

The Beliefs of Israel's Enemies

Despite attempts at political correctness, virtually every militant enemy in the Middle East that opposes Israel adheres to the teachings of Islam. At the same time, many people, including American presidents and political leaders, have declared Islam a religion of peace. But what do Muslims really believe?

The foundational beliefs of Islam have historically been based upon what are known as the five pillars of Islam. These include:

1. Faith or belief in the oneness of God (Allah) and the finality of the prophet-hood of Muhammad;

2. Establishment of the daily prayers;

3. Concern for and almsgiving to the needy;

4. Self-purification through fasting; and

5. The pilgrimage to Makkah (Mecca) for those who are able.[1]

Two main branches of Islam exist today—Sunni and Shia (a third group, Sufi Islam, also exists as a mystical form of Islam). Sunnis comprise about 90 percent of Muslims, and Shia make up most of the remaining world population of Muslims. The main difference between the two groups is a matter of whom they recognize as the true leader of Islam following the death of Muhammad, the founder of Islam. Sunnis believe that the rightful successor of Muhammad was Abu Bakr, the father of his wife Aisha. They follow the Qur'an alone for their teachings. By contrast, Shi'ite Muslims believe some of Muhammad's authority carried on with descendants of Muhammad, beginning with his son-in-law, Ali.

Under Abu Bakr, jihad (which some Muslims consider a sixth pillar of Islam) was the means used to extend Islamic rule from Spain to India. The Arabic term *jihad* means "struggle" and has historically been understood to refer to holy war in the name of Allah, the god of Islam. Jihad serves as the basis for the militant terrorist actions and Arab wars against Israel.

Many jihadists are striving to establish a global caliphate (Muslim nation) through a variety of means. While direct conflict is the most visible means, other Muslim movements focus on *fatah*—the idea of infiltrating a community or nation to the point that Islam has a significant influence. Often called *Islamification* in the West, the shifting demographics of Europe and even some parts of North America testify to how effectively this is taking place. Today, there are even parts of the United Kingdom where Sharia law is practiced, and there are advocates seeking its use in American courts.

Another way that radical Islam is spreading its influence is through indoctrination. Where do tomorrow's militant Muslims join a classroom? Online. Counterterrorism analyst Rohan Gunaratna reported in March 2013, "There are more than 10,000 extremist websites on the Internet compared to fewer than 100 countering them…Terrorists are increasingly exploiting the Internet as a tool for mass communication and radicalization."[2]

Such tactics are clearly working. As of this writing, a *Washington Post* headline announced three American teens, recruited online, who were caught trying to join the Islamic State. According to authorities, "This year alone, officials have detained at least 15 U.S. citizens—nine of them female—who were trying to travel to Syria to join the militants. Almost all of them were Muslims in their teens or early 20s, and almost all were arrested at airports waiting to board flights."[3]

What is the goal? For those pursuing a global caliphate, it's a world ruled by Sharia law, the system of government used in many Muslim-majority countries today. Sharia law is rule by the Qur'an (the holy book of Islam) and the teachings of the Hadith (authoritative commentaries on the words of the Qur'an). Though Muslim nations may vary in how they apply Sharia law, they are rather uniform in recognizing its absolute authority over all of life. According to author Gregory Davis:

> Unlike many religions, Islam includes a mandatory and highly specific legal and political plan for society called Sharia, which translates approximately as "way" or "path." The precepts of Sharia are derived from the commandments of the Quran and the Sunnah (the teachings and precedents of Muhammad as found in the reliable hadiths and the Sira). Together, the Quran and the Sunnah establish the dictates of Sharia, which is the blueprint for the good Islamic society. Because Sharia originates with the Quran and the Sunnah, it is not optional. Sharia is the legal code ordained by Allah for all mankind. To violate Sharia or not to accept its authority is to commit rebellion against Allah, which Allah's faithful are required to combat.
>
> There is no separation between the religious and the political in Islam; rather Islam and Sharia constitute a comprehensive means of ordering society at every level. While it is in theory possible for an Islamic society to have different outward forms—an elective system of

government, a hereditary monarchy, etc.—whatever the outward structure of the government, Sharia is the prescribed content. It is this fact that puts Sharia into conflict with forms of government based on anything other than the Quran and the Sunnah.[4]

There are many harsh examples of the extent of Sharia law's authority. For example, the commands of the Hadith teach, "If a Muslim changes his religion, kill him" (Bukhari 9.57). In other words, any person born a Muslim who changes his or her religion and refuses to recant can be killed. This is indeed how this command is applied today by some Muslim nations. In fact, 47 of the world's 190-plus nations are predominantly Muslim. Of the 16 predominantly Muslim nations in North Africa and the Middle East, not one is a democracy (in contrast with Israel, which is the longest-existing democracy in the Middle East).

In the seventh century, conquered Christians in Syria were forced to sign a surrender treaty called the Pact of Umar. Its commands include several laws applied since in other nations under Muslim rule, which included restrictions on the construction of church buildings, evangelizing Muslims, and public displays of Christian worship. In general, these restrictions were applied as conditions of a covenant of surrender and submission (called *dhimma*) to Muslim overlords.[5] These same restrictions still apply to Christians (and other non-Muslims) in Muslim-dominated countries throughout the Middle East today.

The Qur'an itself prescribes harsh penalties upon non-Muslims. For example, Surah 5:33 states, "The punishment of those who wage war against Allah and His Messenger, and strive with might and main for mischief through the land is: execution, or crucifixion, or the cutting off of hands and feet from opposite sides, or exile from the land."

While social media headlines have recently focused mainly on beheadings at the hands of ISIS, violent punishments are common in societies under Sharia law, and women are especially vulnerable. For example, in 2008, 26-year-old Saudi Fatima Al-Mutairi was executed by her own brother due to her conversion to Christ. Prior to her death, she was locked in a room for four hours. During this time she composed a poem titled "And We for the Sake of Christ All Things Bear." Fatima made this poem public via the Internet just before she died, and a portion of it appears below:

> We left Mohammed, and we do not follow in his path
> We followed Jesus Christ, the Clear Truth
> Truly, we love our homeland, and we are not traitors
> We take pride that we are Saudi citizens
> How could we betray our homeland, our dear people?
> How could we, when for death—for Saudi Arabia—
> we stand ready?
> The homeland of my grandfathers, their glories,
> and odes—for it I am writing
> And we say, "We are proud, proud, proud to be Saudis"
> We chose our way, the way of the rightly guided
> And every man is free to choose any religion
> Be content to leave us to ourselves to be believers in Jesus
> Let us live in grace before our time comes
> There are tears on my cheek, and Oh! the heart is sad
> To those who become Christians, how you are so cruel!
> And the Messiah says, "Blessed are the Persecuted"
> And we for the sake of Christ all things bear
> What is it to you that we are infidels?
> You do not enter our graves, as if with us buried
> Enough—your swords do not concern me,
> not evil nor disgrace
> Your threats do not trouble me, and we are not afraid
> And by God, I am unto death a Christian—Verily
> I cry for what passed by, of a sad life.[6]

The lack of religious freedom in Muslim-majority nations is chilling. As of 2014, there are 13 nations worldwide where "people who openly espouse atheism or reject the official state religion of Islam face execution under the law." Every one of these nations is under some level of Sharia law. The full list includes "Afghanistan, Iran, Malaysia, Maldives, Mauritania, Nigeria, Pakistan, Qatar, Saudi Arabia, Somalia, Sudan, United Arab Emirates and Yemen."[7]

Even blogging can be dangerous business. Blogger Raif Badawi was sentenced to 10 years in prison and 1000 lashings by a Saudi court for "insulting Islam." The content of his website, which debated the role of politics and religion in Saudi life, resulted in a significant punishment by the same government that still refuses to grant women the legal right to drive a car. Raif's words of criticism were interpreted as "terrorism" and resulted in an "extremely harsh" response from the Saudi government.[8]

In Iraq, ISIS terrorists have resorted to turning churches into prisons. According to ChristianPost.com, "Detainees were held at the ancient Chaldean Church of the Immaculate Conception in the eastern part of the city, having been blindfolded and handcuffed. St. George's monastery has also allegedly been used as a female detention centre."[9] Other churches have intentionally been destroyed, including Chaldean Sisters of the Sacred Heart in Mosul. To give some idea of the extent of the problem in Iraq, according to the United Nations, more than 1200 Iraqis were killed by acts of terrorism and violence in November 2014 alone.[10]

Important Clarifying Points

As we cite all of what is happening today, *please note that we are not claiming all Muslims are militants*. Yet from the perspective of Israel, all militants are Muslims. The nation of Israel is not under attack from Christians, Hindus, Buddhists, or atheists. Instead, those who follow a literal, historic interpretation of some of Islam's teachings have taken the lead in opposing Israel.

It's also important to point out two key ways in which the teachings of Islam compare to those of biblical Christianity. First, the god of Islam is *not* the same person as the God of the Bible. Second, the holy book of Islam (the Qur'an) is *not* the same as the holy book of Christianity (the Bible).

The God of Islam Is Not the Same as the God of the Bible

Popular culture and even religious scholars have trended toward focusing on "interfaith initiatives" that de-emphasize the distinctions between different religions. And there are some who say that Allah and the God of the Bible are the same person, by two different names. But is that the case?

While *Allah* is the Arabic word for God, a look at the Qur'an and Islamic teaching reveals he is far different from the God of the Bible. Some of the major differences include:

ALLAH	GOD
Allah is one	One God in three Persons (Father, Son, Holy Spirit)
Jesus is a prophet	Jesus is Lord and the resurrected Savior
The Qur'an is divine	The Bible is God's inspired, inerrant truth
Allah does not have emotional feelings toward people	God loves each person personally

The Holy Book of Islam Is Not the Same as the Holy Book of Christianity

Even a cursory comparison of the Qur'an and Bible reveal that Islam and Christianity are two very different faiths. A few important distinctions include:

QUR'AN	BIBLE
One human author	Approximately 40 authors
Frequently contradicts itself (Muslims call this *abrogation*)	Differences among authors, but no contradictions
Few early copies exist	Thousands of early copies exist
No personal salvation	Salvation found in Jesus Christ alone
Five pillars to earn favor	Grace alone through Christ alone
Eternity uncertain unless one dies as a martyr in jihad	Eternity certain based on Christ's finished work

God loves Muslims and wants to save them. However, the teachings of the Qur'an are incompatible with the teachings of the Bible, and the Qur'an is used to justify the actions of many who seek the destruction of the Jewish people and nation.

The Violence of Radical Islam

The website TheRelgionofPeace.com records more than 24,000 deadly terror attacks by militant Muslims since September 11, 2001, in which thousands of people have been killed. In November 2014 alone, at the time of this writing, statistics noted the following:

- 284 jihad attacks
- 23 countries
- 2515 dead bodies
- 2700 critically injured[11]

And those figures are for just one month. Over time, these numbers add up. All of this carnage cannot be explained away as simply the work of a few fanatical extremists. If Christian extremists were to blame for carrying out even a tiny fraction of such atrocities, the world press would denounce all of Christianity. But when it comes to the actions of Islamic extremists, the press is strangely quiet.

Once again, we do not believe all Muslims are extremists. In fact, most are not. But the problem is that there are at least tens of thousands, if not hundreds of thousands, who are bent on using force and violence to spread their religious beliefs.

Where are the voices from within the Islamic communities around the world calling for reform, restraint, moral sanity, and human decency? And why is the global community—including the UN—largely silent when Islamic extremists call for Israel's annihilation? The reluctance and refusal to condemn the actions of Islamic terrorists only allows them to continue carrying out their agenda.

CHAPTER 3

The Miracle of Israel's Existence

From the start, the fact of Israel's existence can only be described as a miracle. A 99-year-old man named Abraham and his 90-year-old wife, Sarah, became the parents of Isaac, the child the Lord promised to build into a nation. Known originally as Abram ("exalted father"), Abraham was called by God to leave the city of Ur and set out for the land of Canaan, which God promised to give to him and his descendants after him (Genesis 12:1-3).

However, after ten years' residence in Canaan, Abram remained childless and became concerned about a successor. He proposed adopting his chief steward, Eliezer of Damascus, an Aramaean, as his heir (Genesis 15:1-2). But God assured Abram he would have a son of his own as his heir (Genesis 15:4). Abram believed God's promise, and was accounted righteous by God (Genesis 15:6). Abram's faith response was so significant that it is recorded five times in the New Testament as the ultimate example of faith in God (Romans 4:3,9,22; Galatians 3:6; James 2:23).

By the end of the day, God cut a covenant with Abram, promising to give the land of Canaan to his descendants (Genesis 15:18).

He later reaffirmed His covenant with Abram, changing his name to Abraham ("father of a multitude") and emphasizing that the land of Canaan was promised to his descendants through Isaac, the son of Sarah (Genesis 17:1-21). As we read the entire account of the patriarch and his journey of faith, it becomes obvious God deliberately waited to allow Sarah to conceive a son in her old age, even after the age of natural human limitations, so that the Jewish race would begin with a miraculous conception. Then, 2000 years later, God would intervene in human history with an even greater miracle—the virginal conception of Jesus Christ, the incarnate Son of God (Matthew 1:18-25).

The Old Testament focuses on God's covenantal promises to Israel, the nation that descended from Abraham through Isaac and Jacob. At the same time, the Hebrew Scriptures included frequent references to God's love and grace toward Gentiles (non-Jews). For example, Ruth, a Moabite, was converted to the Lord and ended up becoming the great-grandmother of David—Israel's greatest king (Ruth 4:16-22). Joseph married an Egyptian, Asenath, who became the mother of two of the tribes of Israel—Ephraim and Manasseh (Genesis 41:45-52). While dedicating the Jewish temple, Solomon promised that prayers could be offered there by "a foreigner, who is not of Your people Israel" (1 Kings 8:41). The prophet Isaiah described the temple as a "house of prayer for all nations" (Isaiah 56:7), and he predicted that God's light and glory would shine on the Gentiles (Isaiah 62:1-2).

The History of Israel

The Old Testament opens with the stories of the patriarchs (Abraham, Isaac, and Jacob) who received and believed the promises of God. Next it moves to the period of the exodus from Egypt under Moses' leadership. Scripture then continues with the conquest of the Promised Land by Joshua and its settlement in the days of the Judges. Finally, the Hebrew Scriptures take us to the era of the theocratic kingdom—a literal kingdom of God on earth adminis-tered by human rulers under the authority of God. Yet the failure of those rulers eventually led to the invasion and collapse of the north-ern kingdom of Israel in 733 and 722 BC to the Assyrians, and the fall of the southern kingdom of Judah in three stages to Nebuchad-nezzar and the Babylonians from 605 to 586 BC.

From that point until the end of the Old Testament record, the Jewish nation lived largely in subjection to the Babylonians (ancient Iraq) and the Persians (ancient Iran). During the Persian period, Cyrus the Great decreed the Jews could return from the Babylo-nian captivity to rebuild their temple in Jerusalem. And the Old Testament closes with the Jewish people benefiting from the Per-sian benevolence.

Between the Old and New Testaments, both the Greeks and then the Romans dominated the Middle East, including Israel, which was divided into the provinces of Judea, Samaria, and Gal-ilee. As the New Testament opens, Rome rules the world and has appointed its own authorities over the Jewish people. In fact, Jesus Himself is executed in a Roman-style crucifixion ordered by Pon-tius Pilate. After Christ rose from the dead, the disciples received the Great Commission (Matthew 28:19-20) and were empowered on the Day of Pentecost to begin the church (Acts 2). The rest of the New Testament emphasizes the church as a distinct and sepa-rate entity from the nation of Israel. While various Jewish questions remained (such as issues relating to dietary laws, Jews eating with Gentiles, and certain social obligations and religious practices), the New Testament church established a clear identity of its own.

By the end of the New Testament era, there were more Gentiles than Jews within the young but fast-growing church. Eventually Peter and Paul were both executed, and John was later exiled to the island of Patmos, where he received the Revelation (Greek, *Apoc-alypsis*) as the final book of inspired Scripture. From there, Chris-tianity continued to spread into Europe, Asia, and Africa. In the

meantime, Jewish nationalism reached a fervency that led to a rebellion against the Roman overlords. In response, the Roman army
came up against Jerusalem and destroyed it in AD 70.

The Postbiblical History of Israel

Destruction of the Temple (AD 70). Just as Jesus had predicted
four decades earlier, the Romans destroyed the Jewish temple. The
events of AD 70, however, were preceded by other battles. A Jewish
revolt in AD 66 prompted a response from Rome. The first attempt
to quiet the Jewish rebellion ended in failure, so Emperor Nero sent
Vespasian, a Roman general, who successfully attacked Galilee, the
Transjordan, and Idumea, killing thousands of Jewish people along
the way.

But before Vespasian could lay siege to Jerusalem, Nero died, and
Vespasian returned to Rome to lay claim to the throne. After doing
so, Vespasian appointed his son, Titus, in charge of the Roman army.
It was Titus who ended up besieging the city of Jerusalem in AD
70. After several months, the city finally fell, and the Roman troops
destroyed the temple. Sources differ on how many Jewish people
died, but some estimates range from 500,000 to 1,000,000 people.

Interestingly, some of the Christian Jews who lived in Jerusalem
were spared from death because they knew of the impending destruction based on Jesus' prophetic Olivet Discourse as recorded by Luke:

> When you see Jerusalem surrounded by armies, then
> know that its desolation is near. Then let those who are
> in Judea flee to the mountains, let those who are in the
> midst of her depart, and let not those who are in the
> country enter her (Luke 21:20-21).

The Bar Kochba Rebellion (AD 135). Following Emperor Hadrian's announcement that he was going to build a pagan temple on the
site of the Jewish temple ruins and restrict the practice of the Jewish
religion, another Jewish rebellion arose in Jerusalem—this one led

by Simon bar Kochba. Approximately 500,000 people were killed during the fighting and the revolt failed, resulting in the near-total expulsion of Jews from their ancient homeland.

Roman and Byzantine Periods (135–638). Under the direction of the Roman emperor Hadrian, a new city called Aelia Capitolina was built over the ruins of Jerusalem. Jews were forbidden to set foot inside the new city under penalty of death. A pagan temple was also constructed and the name of the province of Judah was changed to Syria Palestina, from which the name *Palestine* was later derived. In 312, the Roman emperor Constantine converted to Christianity and in the decades that followed, the Roman Empire eventually became Christianized. Christianity became the dominant religion in Europe, the Middle East, and North Africa during the era known as the Byzantine Period (324–638). In 330, the capital was moved from Rome to Byzantium, which then was renamed Constantinople.

The Muslim Period (638–1090). During the Muslim conquest of the seventh century, the Middle East came under Muslim rule. Not long after Muhammad's death, his followers conquered Palestine and contact with the West was virtually ended. During this period, the Mosque of Omar (Dome of the Rock) and the al-Aqsa Mosque were built on the Temple Mount, where they have now stood for nearly 1300 years as symbols of Muslim domination and influence. To this very day, the controversy regarding control of the Temple Mount has prevented Jews from rebuilding their own temple on this holy site.

The Crusader Period (1099–1291). During the Crusader period, European Catholic warriors invaded the Holy Land in an attempt to take it back from the Muslims who had desecrated some of the ancient Christian sites, including the tomb of the Holy Sepulcher. Both Muslims and Jews were slaughtered when the overzealous crusaders took Jerusalem and established it as the Latin Kingdom of Jerusalem under the auspices of the Roman Catholic Church. Many people today forget that the city was Christianized for about 100 years, and other parts of Palestine remained under European control for nearly 200 years.

The Saladin and Mamluk Periods (1187–1517). The Syrian Muslim scholar Ali ibn Tahir al-Sulami revived the idea of calling for *jihad* (holy war) to recapture the Holy City from the Crusaders. In response, Saladin rallied 30,000 soldiers in Syria, crossed the Jordan, and overwhelmingly defeated the Crusader force of 20,000 at the Horns of Hittim in Galilee on June 30, 1187. By October 2, Jerusalem surrendered to Saladin after a two-week siege. In the aftermath, the Muslims made a determined effort to re-Islamize Jerusalem. The golden cross of the Crusaders was removed from the al-Aqsa Mosque and the Catholic altar was removed from the Dome of the Rock.

In the years that followed, there were continual conflicts between the Muslims and Crusaders. In 1219, Saladin's nephew, al-Mu'azzam, ordered the destruction of Jerusalem's walls and the depopulation of the city to keep it from the Crusaders. By 1260, the city came under the control of the Mamluks, who came from central Asia.

Ottoman Turkish Period (1517–1917). In 1517, the Mamluks were replaced by the Turks. Under the leadership of Suleiman the Magnificent (1494–1566), Jerusalem was rebuilt as a Turkish Muslim city. During this time, the Islamic influence on the culture of Palestine continued to grow. The rebuilding of Jerusalem's walls was completed in 1566, and these walls still stand today, enclosing the Old City. Despite numerous local conflicts, the Turkish period provided general protection from foreign invasions and ultimately opened contact with the West during the nineteenth century. However, the plight of Israel changed dramatically during World War I, when the Turks allied themselves with Kaiser Wilhelm of Germany. Germany lost the war and the Turks lost control of Palestine to the British, who set up a mandate over the region from 1917–1948.

The British Period. In 1917, Arthur Balfour, foreign secretary of

Great Britain, issued the following statement, known as the Balfour Declaration, in an attempt to gain the support of influential Jews for the war against Germany:

> Dear Lord Rothschild:
>
> I have much pleasure in conveying to you, on behalf of His Majesty's Government, the following declaration of sympathy with Jewish Zionist aspirations which has been submitted to, and approved by, the Cabinet.
>
>> "His Majesty's Government view with favour the establishment in Palestine of a national home for the Jewish people, and will use their best endeavours to facilitate the achievement of this object, it being clearly understood that nothing shall be done which may prejudice the civil and religious rights of existing non-Jewish communities in Palestine, or the rights and political status enjoyed by Jews in any other country."
>
> I should be grateful if you would bring this declaration to the knowledge of the Zionist Federation.
>
> Yours sincerely;
> Arthur James Balfour[1]

The British had grown increasingly impatient in their attempts to mediate the ever-increasing hostilities between the Arabs and Jews who were under their supervision. Nevertheless, it was the United Kingdom's disciplined presence in that tumultuous region that ultimately kept the Arabs from driving the Jews into the sea at a time when they were defenseless and outnumbered.

By 1939, with constant unrest in Palestine, Great Britain began to go back on the Balfour Declaration and instead favor Arab independence and control of the area. Still, Jewish immigration continued, and accelerated during the intense persecution of the Jewish people in Europe under the Nazi regime. By the time the

British relinquished control of the region in 1947, approximately 670,000 Jews lived in the land, and they were now more capable of defending themselves.

The Re-establishment of Modern Israel

For centuries, Christians and Jews have been anticipating a miracle—the re-establishment of the nation of Israel in their ancestral homeland. The reasons behind this anticipation are the numerous prophecies and promises of God recorded throughout the Bible that clearly indicate there would indeed be a Jewish homeland in Israel in the last days. This miracle occurred on May 14, 1948, when the Declaration of the Establishment of the State of Israel was proclaimed.

To understand the significance of this miraculous event, it is necessary to know the history of this land. As a bridge between Asia to the north, Iran to the east, Africa to the south, and the Mediterranean Sea to the west, Israel has long been a battleground for the invading armies of the world.

Nebuchadnezzar of Babylon, Cyrus the Persian, and Alexander the Great all trampled and battled their way across the land that God had originally deeded to the Jews. Eventually, the Romans succeeded in conquering everything west of the Euphrates River from Europe to Africa and were in power at the time of Christ. Since then, history has recorded one conflict after another in the Holy Land.

After 19 centuries of being expelled from the land of Israel, the Jewish people are planted again back in their own homeland. The Bible prophecies regarding future events assume that Israel will exist as a nation in the last days. But for about 19 centuries, there was no nation. There were a few Jewish people who remained in the land, but Israel did not become a nation again until 1948.

The prophet Isaiah, in the final chapter of his book, gives us one of the most amazing prophetic declarations in the entire Bible: "Who has heard such a thing? Who has seen such things? Shall the earth be made to give birth in one day? Or shall a nation be born at once? For as soon as Zion was in labor, she gave birth to her children" (Isaiah 66:8).

Both Christian and Jewish scholars acknowledge this passage as a prediction of Israel's rebirth in the land instantaneously, a nation born in a day. This has never happened before in all of history. Never has a nation or a group of people who were expelled from their land returned after nearly 2000 years with their language, their heritage, and their commitments largely intact.

The very fact that Israel exists today is evidence of the fact that Bible prophecy is true and can be trusted. It demonstrates that God keeps His promises and that He has the power to fulfill what He has said will happen in the future. The return of Israel is a super sign of the end times. It is one event that should cause us to respond, "The prophecy has already been fulfilled. Israel has returned."

But what if the Jews are expelled from the land again because of unbelief? According to the Bible, this will not occur. We read in the Bible that God will bring the people of Israel back to the land and plant them there permanently, never to be removed again (Isaiah 11:11-12). Their first return took place at the end of the Babylonian captivity, and the Jewish people were scattered again when the Romans destroyed Jerusalem in AD 70. The second return had its beginnings in the late nineteenth century and became more and more sizeable through the twentieth century. This alone should capture our attention and tell us we are moving closer to the time of the end.

The prophet Ezekiel also spoke of this future rebirth of Israel. His prophecies clearly note Israel's return to life, its return to the land, and the nation's eventual return to the Lord.

Return to Life

In the book of Ezekiel we read of a time when the nation of Israel would one day return to life. Note what God said:

> I will take you from among the nations, gather you out
> of all countries, and bring you into your own land. Then

> I will sprinkle clean water on you, and you shall be clean;
> I will cleanse you from all your filthiness and from all
> your idols. I will give you a new heart and put a new
> spirit within you; I will take the heart of stone out of
> your flesh and give you a heart of flesh. I will put My
> Spirit within you and cause you to walk in My statutes,
> and you will keep My judgments and do them. Then
> you shall dwell in the land that I gave to your fathers;
> you shall be My people, and I will be your God (Eze-
> kiel 36:24-28).

Ezekiel wrote this at a time when the Babylonians had devas-
tated the southern kingdom, and when the prophet himself had
been taken into captivity. Yet he said there would come a time when
a nation that appeared to be dead would come back to life under the
providence and care of God. God has not abandoned His people.
He still has a plan and a purpose for them and for their future.

Then in Ezekiel chapter 37 we come to the famous prediction
regarding the valley of the dry bones: "The hand of the LORD came
upon me and brought me out in the Spirit of the LORD, and set me
down in the midst of the valley; and it was full of bones" (Ezekiel
37:1). The bones symbolize the nation and people of Israel, which
appear to be dead and are scattered throughout the world. "Then
He caused me to pass by them all around, and behold, there were
very many in the open valley; and indeed they were very dry" (verse
2). In other words, they had been there for a long time. "And He said
to me, 'Son of man, can these bones live?' So I answered, 'O Lord
GOD, You know'" (verse 3). What is the answer? "Again He said to
me, 'Prophesy to these bones, and say to them, "O dry bones, hear
the word of the LORD!" ' " (Ezekiel 37:4).

Then Ezekiel went on to say that as he preached to the bones,
there was a rattling sound, and the bones began to come together.
The old spiritual, "Dry Bones," which speaks of bones being joined
together, comes from this very passage of Scripture, in which the
bones of the skeletons suddenly begin to assemble right in front of

the eyes of the prophet. Ezekiel noted that when the bones came together, flesh and sinews formed on them, but there was no breath in them—no spiritual life (verses 7-8). Then we read this:

> He said to me, "Prophesy to the breath, prophesy, son of man, and say to the breath, 'Thus says the Lord GOD: "Come from the four winds, O breath, and breathe on these slain, that they may live."'" So I prophesied as He commanded me, and breath came into them, and they lived, and stood upon their feet, an exceedingly great army (verses 9-10).

While Ezekiel was preaching to dry bones in a desert valley, they came together and stood up. But there was no life in them—not until the breath of God entered them. At that point they suddenly became alive not only physically, but also spiritually. Then God explained the meaning of the vision, saying to Ezekiel, "Son of man, these bones are the whole house of Israel."

Ezekiel chapter 37, then, is clearly a prophecy about Israel's future destiny. This is not a prophecy about the church. And we are seeing this prophecy come to fruition as the people of Israel return to their land and the "bones" are being reassembled. This nation has returned to life physically, and there is coming a day when it will return to life spiritually. That's what God's Word tells us.

Return to the Land

The all-important question about Israel's return is this: Does God's promise of this return mean that His blessings will return as well? Or will the people of Israel continue to face the difficulties and challenges that they have always faced throughout their history? In other words, what is ahead for the nation and its people?

The prediction of Israel's return to the land is one of the great prophecies of the Old Testament. Yet for centuries, some people said, "Oh, they'll never go back. They're scattered all over the world."

However, the Jewish people themselves understood God's

promise, which is clearly stated in Isaiah chapter 11. There, the prophet looked down through the corridors of history, into the distant future, and spoke of the millennial kingdom. He prophesied of the coming Messiah as a descendant of Jesse, David's father. The prophet also described the sevenfold Spirit of the Lord resting on the Messiah: "There shall come forth a rod from the stem of Jesse, and a Branch shall grow out of his roots. The spirit of the LORD shall rest upon Him, the spirit of wisdom and understanding, the spirit of counsel and might, the spirit of knowledge and of the fear of the LORD" (Isaiah 11:1-2).

This is the sevenfold plentitude of the Spirit of God, the seven spirits that are referred to in Revelation 1:4. In the symbolism of the book of Revelation, the seven spirits were there before the throne of God. These are not seven Holy Spirits. There is only one Holy Spirit. But Isaiah presented a sevenfold description of the Spirit, saying that the Spirit is the Spirit of the Lord, of wisdom and understanding, of counsel and might, of the fear of the Lord, and so on. What this tells us is that God would do something spiritually powerful. The "Branch" that comes "from the stem of Jesse" is a reference to the Messiah. He will come forth, in the future, out of the root of Jesse and David. The promised Savior, Jesus the Messiah, would be a descendant of King David.

Isaiah 11:4 then says this about the Messiah: "With righteousness He shall judge the poor, and decide with equity for the meek of the earth; He shall strike the earth with the rod of His mouth, and with the breath of His lips He shall slay the wicked." This is the very same picture we have of Jesus Christ in the book of Revelation: There is coming a day when He will physically return to the earth, and He will reign with fairness and justice.

During Messiah's reign, the wolf, the lamb, the lion, and the calf will all lie down with one another—the millennial kingdom will be a time of peace and prosperity (Isaiah 11:6-8). Isaiah then says, "And in that day there shall be a Root of Jesse, who shall stand as a banner to the people; for the Gentiles shall seek Him, and His resting place shall be glorious" (Isaiah 11:10). "The people" is a reference to the Jews, and "the nations" refers to the Gentiles. In other words, the Savior is coming for both the Jews and the Gentiles. He is the banner of God's love over both of them. He is the One who calls both of them to faith in the Lord God Himself.

Then we come to the key verse: "It shall come to pass in that day that the Lord shall set His hand again the second time to recover the remnant of His people who are left" (Isaiah 11:11). Where will God recover His people from? According to the rest of verse 11, they will come from Assyria, Egypt, Pathros, Cush, Elam, Shinar, and other places—that is, modern-day Africa, Iraq, Iran, and other places.

As we said earlier, this return has been going on for some time and continues on through today. They are part of the *aliya* (the Hebrew term for "return"), the regathering to the Promised Land itself. Many of them see themselves as fulfilling Isaiah's prophecy.

For Jewish readers of this book, let us share a word with you for a moment, from our hearts to yours. God has called you to be a unique people unto Himself. He has blessed you and sustained you through great difficulties as a nation over the centuries. But He is also calling you to faith in Himself. It is not enough to say, "We'll rebuild the nation by our own political prowess, our own military might, and our own intellectual ingenuity." While God may use those things, ultimately, there is more. Only if the Lord builds the house will it stand. If He doesn't, it will not.

People frequently ask us, "Don't you think Israel could suffer devastation and judgment again and be scattered once more?" Humanly speaking, anything might be possible. But spiritually speaking, we believe the Bible makes it very clear that once the Jewish people are gathered a second time, they will never be scattered again. Israel will remain in the land.

There are biblical predictions that talk about war in the Middle East, and about Israel being chased into the wilderness. According to Scripture, the Jewish people will face more difficulties in the days to come. But the Abrahamic Covenant is an unconditional promise. God is fulfilling that promise now, and He will never go back on it.

And there's more. Bible prophecy tells us that not only will the Jewish people return to the land and return to life, but that they will also return to the Lord.

Return to the Lord

The prophecies of the rebirth of the nation of Israel center on three elements: the people's return to the land, their return to life, and ultimately, their return to the Lord Himself. That may sound strange to Jewish people. They would respond, "We've always believed in the Lord God, Yahweh Himself, the God of Israel, the God of Abraham and Isaac and Jacob." While that is true intellectually and theologically, the real issue is, Do you really believe in Him personally, spiritually? Is He Lord and God and Savior in your life on a personal basis?

As we read the Old Testament, the Hebrew Scriptures, we discover that there were times when the people of Israel loved the Lord their God and followed Him, and there were times when they did not. When they turned away from God, they came under His judgment.

Another important Bible passage that speaks of Israel's return to the land is found in Ezekiel chapter 20. Notice what God said through the prophet Ezekiel with regard to the distant future: "I will bring you out from the peoples and gather you out of the countries where you are scattered, with a mighty hand, with an outstretched arm, and with fury poured out" (verse 34). God was saying, "I will do this powerfully. I will do it dramatically." Then He said, "I will bring you into the wilderness of the peoples, and there I will plead My case with you face to face" (verse 35).

Why will God plead with His own people face-to-face? Because of His concern over their heart, their attitude, and their relationship to Him. He goes on to say, "I will purge the rebels from among you, and those who transgress against Me; I will bring them out of the country where they dwell, but they shall not enter the land of Israel. Then you will know that I am the LORD" (verse 38). In summary, Ezekiel foresaw a time when God would spiritually convert the people of Israel and change their heart, soul, and life. And when that happens, He will also purge the rebels from among them. Verse 42 goes on to describe the result: "Then you shall know that I am the LORD, when I bring you into the land of Israel, into the country for which I raised My hand in an oath to give to your fathers."

There is coming a day of grace from God Himself. He makes this promise to the people in verses 43-44:

> There you shall remember your ways and all your doings with which you were defiled; and you shall loathe yourselves in your own sight because of all the evils that you have committed. Then you shall know that I am the LORD, when I have dealt with you for My name's sake, not according to your wicked ways nor according to your corrupt doings, O house of Israel.

To those who will respond to the grace of God, He says, "I will be your Lord. I will be your God. I will save you. I will cleanse you. I will change you. I will not deal with you according to your past failures. I will deal with you by giving you a new heart and a new spirit, and then making with you a New Covenant, a New Agreement."

Jesus, who Himself was Jewish, dared to say at His Last Supper, "The cup that I am drinking represents the blood of the New Covenant. Just as the blood of animals was shed for your sins in the Old Testament, My blood is shed for you now." If Jesus was nothing more than a Jewish human being, He could not atone for His own sins, let alone atone for the sins of others. But He really was the Son of God, God incarnate in human flesh. He was the fulfillment of the Old Testament prophecies that said, "One day your God will come to you." That comes right out of Isaiah chapter 40. How else can God literally come to us unless He comes in human flesh? Jesus was God in sandals, God on foot. He walked among us, and He now lives above us and points us to the way of salvation.

The Old Testament repeatedly communicated the fact that the coming Messiah was going to die. He would be killed and cut off. That's the message of Isaiah chapter 53. It's the message of Daniel chapter 9. If the Messiah was going to be cut off and killed, how could He reign unless He was resurrected? And how could He be resurrected unless He is the Divine Son of God Himself?

It is no mere human being who is going to establish the greatness of Israel in the future. No, it is the Son of God Himself. That is why Jesus came. He came to be the Savior, the banner, the ensign, for Jews and Gentiles alike, to call all of us to faith in the Lord God of the Bible, the God Jehovah, the Creator God who made us in His own image and likeness, so that we might have a relationship with Him.

CHAPTER 4

Israel's Divine Purpose

Three days before Jesus was crucified in Jerusalem, He wept over the city and the Hebrew people for rejecting Him. We read His lament in Matthew 23:37-39:

> O Jerusalem, Jerusalem, the one who kills the prophets and stones those who are sent to her! How often I wanted to gather your children together, as a hen gathers her chicks under her wings, but you were not willing! See! Your house is left to you desolate; for I say to you, you shall see Me no more till you say, "Blessed is He who comes in the name of the LORD!"

The fact that the disciples only partly understood what was about to happen is seen by the statement they made after Jesus led them to the Mount of Olives. From there they would have had a clear view across the Kidron Valley at the temple that had been newly rebuilt by Herod. These unlearned fishermen and others from the distant country region of Galilee were evidently quite impressed with "the temple buildings," which they pointed out to Jesus (Matthew

24:1). The temple itself was likely the most elegant and largest build-ing they had ever seen, and they may have assumed it would also impress Jesus. They still did not fully understand He was the Cre-ator of all things!

It is difficult to understand why after three years of watching Jesus teach, perform numerous miracles, and even raise Lazarus from the dead the disciples still didn't truly understand who He was. He was the Son of God who had created the entire world and everything in it. Paul, a theologian well trained in the Old Testa-ment, wrote of Jesus:

> He is the image of the invisible God, the firstborn over all creation. For by Him all things were created that are in heaven and that are on earth, visible and invisible, whether thrones or dominions or principalities or pow-ers. All things were created through Him and for Him. And He is before all things, and in Him all things con-sist. And He is the head of the body, the church, who is the beginning, the firstborn from the dead, that in all things He may have the preeminence.

> For it pleased the Father that in Him all the fullness should dwell, and by Him to reconcile all things to Himself, by Him, whether things on earth or things in heaven, having made peace through the blood of His cross (Colossians 1:15-20).

Within days after Jesus had ridden into Jerusalem on a borrowed donkey to the cries of "Hosanna...Blessed is He who comes in the name of the LORD" (Matthew 21:9), He wept over that Holy City of God. The Jewish leaders (mainly the Sadducees and Pharisees) peti-tioned the Roman government to crucify Him. These religious lead-ers scorned their long-promised Messiah by rejecting His Word, His miracles, and His heavenly Father, and set out to kill Him.

Because the Jewish nation was under Roman rule, it was illegal for the Jewish religious leaders to carry out capital punishment on their own. Instead, they had to appeal to the Roman governing authorities. What's more, Jesus had come to Jerusalem for the annual observance of Passover. The city was filled to overflowing with Jewish people who were there to offer up animal sacrifices for their sins. Very soon, Jesus would offer Himself up as the ultimate sacrifice—He would shed His blood for the sins of the world. As we will see later, the sin of rejecting the Messiah would cost the Jewish nation dearly. In AD 70, the Romans besieged and overcame Jerusalem and destroyed the temple, fulfilling Jesus' prediction that "not one stone shall be left here upon another" (Matthew 24:2).

Jesus' Predictions in Matthew 24

Jesus' impassioned remorse over the growing rejection of Him by His own people as the one and only Savior reveals the importance of the Olivet Discourse. Nationally, the leaders of the nation were fixated on the future Messiah to come as the Son of David. Their assumption was that this leader would overturn the tyrannical Roman government and set up the kingdom of God on earth that is yet to come. They had little interest in a Messiah or "Christ" who would die as a sacrifice for their sins. They were not seeking forgiveness and eternal life in a yet-future kingdom. Their interest was in political, social, cultural, and religious freedom from their Roman overlords right then.

Thankfully, Jesus came to offer real and lasting salvation (John 3:16). As Isaiah 9:6 predicts, there is coming a day when the government will be upon His shoulders and, as Revelation 19:16 says, He will be the King of kings and Lord of lords. This will happen after His glorious appearing, which was described by the apostle John in the book of Revelation, which he wrote around AD 95 while imprisoned on the Isle of Patmos. John describes the entire event in more detail after stating in Revelation 19:10 that "Jesus is the Spirit of prophecy." Then he described one of the most awesome events in the entire Bible—the glorious appearing of Jesus Christ, which will precede His setting up the millennial kingdom.

With regard to Jesus, the Bible speaks of two different comings. The first time, He came to earth born of a virgin so that blood within His veins was the pure blood of God untouched by Adam's nature and sin. Because of this He was able to serve as the perfect sacrifice for the sins of the whole world. As the Old Testament says, God required that a sacrificial lamb be without spot or blemish. The second time, Jesus will come to establish the millennial kingdom spoken of by Daniel and other Hebrew prophets.

We believe Jesus' Olivet Discourse is the greatest end-time prophecy in the entire Bible. It is no accident that all three of the Synoptic Gospels reported it (Matthew 24–25, Mark 13:3-37, and Luke 21:5-24). Such repetition indicates the discourse's great significance. In addition, its source is Jesus, the greatest man who ever lived—God in human flesh. No wonder this message contains more detailed information about the time from Jesus' resurrection to His judgment against all of mankind at His second coming. He stops there, leaving details about both the millennial kingdom and eternity, to be revealed 60 years later to the disciple "whom Jesus loved" (John 20:2), the apostle John. We find these details in the last volume of the great library of God, the book of Revelation.

Jesus' Predictions Regarding the Temple

After the disciples pointed out the grandeur of the temple, Jesus predicted it would be totally destroyed, and His prophecy was fulfilled just 40 years later. As the disciples sat with Jesus on the Mount of Olives, He said to them, "Do you not see all these things? Assuredly, I say to you, not one stone shall be left here upon another, that shall not be thrown down" (Matthew 24:2). In response, the disciples asked three questions: When will this happen? What will be the sign of your coming? And that of the end of the age? (verse 3).

When the Roman general Titus and his armies invaded Jerusalem, he initially gave the order for the soldiers not to destroy the temple. However, as fires spread throughout the city and rose upward to the Temple Mount, the heat became so intense that the gold overlays on the temple walls melted into the cracks between the stones that made up the building. The Roman soldiers who were pillaging the city wanted to get to this gold, so they tore the stones apart—thus fulfilling Jesus' prophecy that not one stone would be left upon another.

This precise fulfillment of prophecy assures us that every prediction that comes from the Lord will come to pass exactly as described. We can know with certainty that what Jesus told us about the future will happen exactly as He predicted. What's more, every prophecy uttered by Jesus fits perfectly with those proclaimed by all the other prophets and writers in both the Old and New Testaments, including Isaiah, Ezekiel, Daniel, Peter, and John.

A few verses later, Jesus gave three more prophecies, all of which have been fulfilled and are still being fulfilled: "They will deliver you up to tribulation and kill you, and you will be hated by all nations for My name's sake" (Matthew 24:9). From the time of Jesus' resurrection up through today, the followers of Jesus have been hated, persecuted, and betrayed. And we can expect that to continue.

In addition, false prophets will come and deceive many. Numerous false cults and religions are masquerading as Christian movements. However, they do not accept the Savior as the only begotten Son of God, and therefore are not part of "the faith which was once for all delivered to the saints" (Jude 3). Because of these false teachers "the love of many will grow cold," just as Jesus predicted (Matthew 24:12).

Yet God never leaves His children without hope. In verse 13, Jesus said, "He who endures to the end shall be saved." The word translated "saved" here should read from the original Greek text as "delivered" rather than "saved." That is, those who miss the rapture and end up going into the Tribulation period yet come to accept

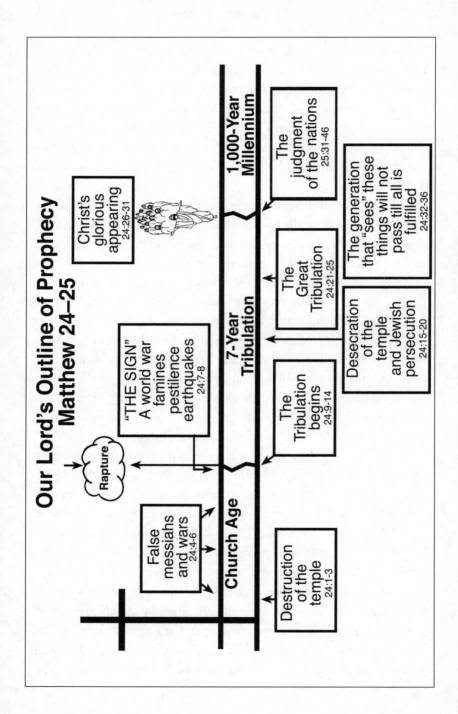

Christ as Savior and refuse the mark of the Antichrist (Revelation 13:16-17) will be delivered if they remain faithful or endure to the end. It is these surviving Tribulation saints who will enter the millennial kingdom in their earthly bodies, marry others, and give birth to children who are part of the largest population explosion in world history.

During this time will come the fulfillment of the many promises to Israel that the populace would increase more than the sands of the sea or the stars of the heavens and that Jesus will be the King of kings and rule over the whole world. The number of God-fearing Jews may equal the entire Gentile population during Jesus' 1000-year kingdom. Why? Because those population promises to Israel have yet to be fulfilled! Even today the Jewish people number only about 0.2 percent of the world's population.

The Sign That Brings on the End

In His sermon about the last days, Jesus said, "This gospel of the kingdom will be preached in all the world as a witness to all the nations, and then the end will come" (Matthew 24:14). This "gospel" is defined by Paul in 1 Corinthians 15:3-8:

> I delivered to you first of all that which I also received: that Christ died for our sins according to the Scriptures, and that He was buried, and that He rose again the third day according to the Scriptures, and that He was seen by Cephas, then by the twelve. After that He was seen by over five hundred brethren at once, of whom the greater part remain to the present, but some have fallen asleep. After that He was seen by James, then by all the apostles. Then last of all He was seen by me also, as by one born out of due time.

There is only one gospel—it has never changed, and never will. Anyone who changes this message is a false prophet or teacher. The gospel is also called "the good news," for it alone offers the salvation from sin that people so desperately need. Without it, there is no way of salvation (Acts 4:12). It is the gospel that we are commanded to preach to every person as a witness to all the nations, "and then the end shall come."

It is clear we have not reached "the end" yet, but we are very close, and it could happen in our lifetime! A key reason this could be the case is because of how far and wide the gospel has spread worldwide. One of the most unforgettable men of faith I (Tim) have ever met was Dr. Cameron Townsend, the founder of Wycliffe Bible Translators. I was a young pastor just out of college in the early 1950s when he came to my church on the outskirts of Minneapolis, Minnesota, for a mission conference. He spoke of how, in the early 1930s, he started training two young missionary Bible translators in a barn in Oklahoma. These trainees sat on nail kegs as he taught them. His vision then was "only 2000 tongues [languages] to go!" Many years later, during my 25 years as a pastor in San Diego, California, I was amazed when my secretary said, "Dr. Townsend of Wycliffe Bible Translators was here to see you." By then, in the mid-1970s, he was a legend of the faith for raising up thousands of young men and women to learn his technique of translating the Bible into the languages of the nations. If a nation didn't have a written language, he taught the missionaries how to make one.

Typical of his giant faith, he wanted help to raise the $25,000 necessary to buy a twin-engine airplane. A pilot in our church served on his national board and had found a plane considered safe for flying missionaries and supplies to the dense jungles in Central and South America. Our church was in the middle of a building program at the time, and I had just returned from a national board meeting with Youth for Christ. At that time, my comments were quite negative regarding our ability to help.

Dr. Townsend didn't even hear me! We prayed together, he thanked me for "[my] encouragement," which I still don't remember, and two weeks later he invited me to pray at the public dedication of his completely debt-free airplane in Balboa City Park. When he introduced me I couldn't believe he thanked me for my "encouragement." To my shame, I left that service asking God for forgiveness for my unbelief and found myself praying to share in "Uncle Cam's great faith."

Today there are still a number of tribes and nations that have yet to receive the Bible in their own language. However, there are multiplied millions in formerly unreached tribes that have now been introduced to the Bible in their own language. Through God's Word, many have been introduced to the Savior, Jesus Christ.

We have not reached all the nations yet, but thanks to many men and women of faith and zeal, the gospel continues to spread. We are getting closer and closer to having the gospel available in every language. So we would do well to pay heed to Jesus' words in His discourse to the disciples: "Watch therefore, for you do not know what hour your Lord is coming…be ready, for the Son of Man is coming at an hour you do not expect…Watch therefore, for you know neither the day nor the hour in which the Son of man is coming" (Matthew 24:42,44; 25:13).

In His message about the last days, Jesus spoke of how difficult that time would be. He warned of deception, wars, famines, earthquakes, and pestilences that would increase in intensity (Matthew 24:4-8). Then in verse 14, He shared the good news that the gospel would go out to all the nations. The spread of the good news as a witness to God's love and mercy to all the nations through radio, television, and digital technology will make it abundantly clear that "the end will come" shortly. The "end" here means the rapture of all believers to the Father's house (John 14:1-3) and the beginning of the seven-year Tribulation.

It is interesting that in both Mark and Luke's coverage of this discourse, Jesus showed His deep concern for the saints who would be present when the temple was abominably desecrated and ultimately destroyed, which happened in AD 70, just as Jesus said it would. This judgment from God, carried out through the Roman government, was due to Israel's rejection of the Messiah.

What is difficult to understand when first studying this part of Jesus' discourse is how the citizens of Jerusalem could have escaped the Roman armies after they had completely surrounded and laid siege to the city. In Matthew 24:15-19, Jesus said,

> "When you see the 'abomination of desolation,' spoken of by Daniel the prophet, standing in the holy place" (whoever reads, let him understand), "then let those who are in Judea flee to the mountains. Let him who is on the housetop not go down to take anything out of his house. And let him who is in the field not go back to get his clothes. But woe to those who are pregnant and to those who are nursing babies in those days!"

Historians indicate that when the Roman army surrounded the city and it was obvious the city was doomed, General Vespasian was called to make an emergency trip to Rome to become the new Caesar because the emperor had died. So Vespasian ordered his troops to withdraw while still retaining the siege of the city. Then he appointed his son Titus to finish the capture and destruction of Jerusalem.

It was during this limited withdrawal by the Roman army that those who took Jesus' warning literally were able to escape and flee to safety. Those who mistakenly thought the withdrawal was permanent were later killed when Jerusalem fell. Those who took Jesus' prophecy literally were saved. Those who did not were lost.

The Disciples' Three Big Questions

The disciples, still confused about Jesus' role in history, could hardly wait to ask Him questions. Evidently they too held to the general prevailing notion that when the Messiah came, He would throw off the cruel yoke of the Roman oppressors and set up God's kingdom. Instead, Jesus was talking about His impending death.

Keep in mind that during three years of ministry with Jesus, they had seen Him do the most incredible miracles anyone had ever done, including raise the dead three times. Their assumption was that if He was the Messiah, then surely His kingdom would come soon. They knew the Old Testament prophets had predicted the Messiah would come in power and set up God's kingdom on earth. Instead, here He was, predicting that He would soon die. Like many others, the disciples had paid little attention to the 109 Old Testament prophecies about Jesus' first coming, which say that He would come to save people from their sins.

In fact, the disciples were so fixated on Jesus' coming to establish God's kingdom that they were blind to His upcoming death and resurrection even though He had predicted these things multiple times. In spite of their confusion, they had enough faith to ask three very important questions: (1) Tell us, when will these things be? (2) What will be the sign of your coming? and (3) What will be the sign of the end of the age?

The Olivet Discourse answers these three specific questions and more. That is why we believe it is the most important end-time prophecy in Scripture. We will continue our discussion of these three questions in the next chapter.

CHAPTER 5

Answering the Three Key Questions

The first words out of the Savior's mouth about the church age as He answered the disciples' three questions were "Take heed that no one deceives you. For many will come in My name saying 'I am the Christ,' and will deceive many" (Matthew 24:4-5). And they have—by the tens of thousands and increasing as we approach the end of the age.

False Christs and Messiahs

History has not lacked for examples of our Lord's prophecy that in the last days (beginning with Pentecost) Christians should "take heed that no one deceives you." In my (Tim's) prophecy-based fiction series Babylon Rising, coauthor Dr. Bob Phillips included the names of some classic examples:

AD 30	Theudas
AD 30	Judas the Galilean
2nd century	Simon Bar Kokhba
5th century	Moses of Crete

AD 591	Wandering Preacher
AD 720	Abu Isa from Baghdad
8th century	Aldebert
AD 832	Moses-Risen from the Dead
AD 1110	Tanchelm of Antwerp
12th century	David Aloroy
AD 1240	Abraham of Ahulfia
AD 1523	David Reubeni
AD 1542	Hayyim Vital
AD 1543	Isaac Luria
AD 1626	Shabbatai Zevi
AD 1726	Jacob Frank
AD 1774	Ann Lee
AD 1792	Richard Brothers
AD 1800	Baal Shem Tov
AD 1919	Father Divine
AD 1959	Maitreya
AD 1993	Ca Van Lieng
AD 1993	Aum Shinn Kyo
AD 1997	Marshall Applewhite
AD 1997	Sun Myung Moon
AD 1998	Nancy Fowler
AD 1998	Hon-Ming Chen
AD 2000	Wayne Bent
AD 2004	Alan John Miller
AD 2013	Moses Hlongwane

It is interesting that no one person has ever been impersonated or called "the Christ" more frequently than Jesus of Nazareth. Yet rarely do they call themselves Jesus. Instead, they use His special designation "the Christ," meaning "the Anointed One" or "the Messiah." All who make such claims have one thing in common: They are false prophets who were inspired by Satan and his fallen demon angels. Knowing this, we should heed Jesus' warning that they will increase in number as we draw closer to the end of the age.

How Not to Be Deceived

If you know and believe the most authentic narration of Jesus' life as given in the four Gospels, it is not difficult to avoid being deceived about the identity of the real Christ or Messiah. Answer for yourself the following questions of anyone who claims to be the Christ:

1. Did he fulfill all 109 Bible messianic prophecies of the Old Testament? *Jesus did!*

2. Was he born of a virgin Hebrew woman—in Bethlehem? *Jesus was!*

3. Was he the greatest teacher in world history? *Jesus was!*

4. Did he live a sinless life? *Jesus did!*

5. Was he crucified, not for his own sins but the sins of the world? *Jesus was!*

6. Did he rise from the dead three days after the crucifixion as he promised multiple times during his lifetime? *Jesus did!*

7. Did God the Father raise him from the dead, proving He approved of the perfect sacrifice for humanity's sin? (Romans 1:4). *True of Jesus!*

8. Was he seen in human form by over 500 people during 40 days on earth after his resurrection before ascending to heaven? *Jesus was!*

9. Did all who testified that they saw, heard, and ate with him willingly die a martyr's death for him? *True of Jesus!*

10. Is he revered, worshipped, and honored by more people today than anyone who ever lived? *Jesus is!*

11. Is he the only way to heavenly peace with God the Father? *Jesus is!*

12. Who in the entire Bible fulfilled Isaiah's messianic prophecy—which Jesus quoted in Luke 4:18—that Messiah would bring "recovery of sight to the blind," as he did with Bartimaeus in Mark 10:52? Not Enoch, Noah, Job, Samuel, or Moses. *Only Jesus!* And He restored eyesight to blind eyes at least eight times! No wonder He could say, "Believe Me for the sake of the works [miracles] themselves" (John 14:11). As we have seen, Jesus' works put Him in a category all by Himself.

No one else in history has had so many imitators as Jesus Christ, which is just one of many irrefutable proofs of His true identity as the one and only Messiah of the world. Even the seventh-century Islamic Mahdi doesn't come close. And that is just one of the 109 prophecies concerning the Messiah that Jesus fulfilled! (Note: The complete list of these prophecies is found in the *Tim LaHaye Prophecy Study Bible* on pages 1559-1563.) Note, however, Jesus' advice when you see the signs of the last days appearing: "See that you are not troubled; for all these things must come to pass, but the end is not yet" (Matthew 24:6).

The Fulfillment of Messianic Prophecy

When Jesus asked His disciples, "Who do men say that I, the Son of Man, am?" He followed their answer with the most important question that could ever be asked: "Who do *you* say that I am?" (Matthew 16:13-14). Here, He brought us all face-to-face with the question that, when answered, determines where we will spend eternity. Our prayer ought to be that everyone can answer with Peter and say, "You are the Christ, the Son of the living God" (verse 16). Peter did not think up that answer on his own. Even though he had lived alongside Jesus for more than three years, had heard Him preach to vast crowds, and had witnessed the healings of many, it was God the Father who revealed to Peter the answer given in Matthew 16:16.

Today we have even more reason to believe that Jesus was the "only begotten Son" of God (John 3:16). We can look at the 109 messianic prophecies Jesus fulfilled during His lifetime that prove beyond all doubt that He alone was and is God's Son. For Jesus of Nazareth is the only person who ever lived who healed every person He met who was in need of healing. As a healer, He stands in a category all by Himself. As Matthew said, "When Jesus went out He saw a great multitude; and He was moved with compassion for them, and healed their sick" (14:14). No man has ever been able to heal as Jesus did.

Jesus' Fulfillment of All 109 Messianic Prophecies

Space does not permit listing all the prophecies Jesus fulfilled during His brief time on earth. However, the following examples are more than enough to prove beyond a shadow of doubt that He is the one and only Messiah:

- Bible prophecy said He would be born of a virgin, without a human father (Isaiah 7:14). The fulfillment is recorded in Matthew 1:22-23 and Luke 2:6-7.

- Seven hundred years before Jesus' birth, the Bible said he would be born in Bethlehem (Micah 5:2). This prophecy was fulfilled (see Matthew 2:1-6), and contains an added miracle within it. When Mary was close to giving birth, she had to travel from Nazareth to Bethlehem, a journey of 70 miles over primitive roads and rough terrain. Amazingly, she did not give birth before arriving in Bethlehem—a miracle in and of itself.

- In Hosea 11:1, God said, "Out of Egypt I called My son." This prophecy declared that at some point, Jesus would be brought "out of Egypt." When King Herod became fearful in response to the wise men, who called little Jesus "He who has been born King of the Jews" (Matthew 2:2), he ordered all the little male children in Bethlehem to be killed. Thus Joseph fled to Egypt with Mary and Jesus (Matthew 2:13-15). After Herod died, Joseph brought Mary and Jesus back from Egypt. In doing so, he fulfilled Hosea 11:1.

- Isaiah 61 predicted Jesus would have a healing ministry (verse 1). Hundreds of years later, Jesus quoted this passage in a synagogue in Nazareth (Luke 4:16-19), then said, "Today this Scripture is fulfilled in your hearing" (verse 21).

- There are more than 50 prophecies having to do with Jesus' death and resurrection, and every single one was fulfilled perfectly. For example:

   1. He was betrayed for 30 pieces of silver (Zechariah 11:12; Matthew 26:15).

   2. He was betrayed by a friend (Psalm 41:9; Luke 22:47).

   3. He was slain between two thieves (Isaiah 53:12; Matthew 27:38).

And the list goes on…

The amazing thing is that Jesus fulfilled all 109 messianic prophecies that would clearly point to Him as the one and only Son of God. That it is legitimate to use such fulfilled prophecies in order to verify His identity is seen in the conversation Jesus had with the two disciples on the road to Emmaus following His resurrection. They were returning home, greatly discouraged after His crucifixion, and He said to them:

"Ought not the Christ to have suffered these things and

to enter into His glory?" And beginning at Moses and all the Prophets, He expounded to them in all the Scriptures the things concerning Himself (Luke 24:26-27).

Later the two disciples returned to Jerusalem and said to one another, "Did not our heart burn within us while He talked with us on the road, and while He opened the Scriptures to us?" (Luke 24:32). I have found that studying the prophecies Jesus fulfilled gives us a warm heart toward Him and His Father.

No One Else Comes Even Close

Not a single one of the 13 billion or so people who have lived on earth could even come close to fulfilling the 109 prophecies that Jesus did. Being born a male child immediately cuts the possibilities roughly in half. Being born in the lineage of David cuts it down many times more, and being born in the little town of Bethlehem after a 70-mile journey cuts it down even further. There may be some who claim to have fulfilled 5 or 6 of the 109 prophecies, but Jesus fulfilled all 109! Jesus fulfilled all the predictions required of Him, confirming that He is the promised Messiah of God. No one else comes even close!

Jesus' Warning to "Take Heed"

These are only some of the many things we can take heed to in order to determine who the Christ of God is. Not only does Jesus Christ alone fulfill all these prophetic requirements for the Son of God—no one else comes even close. Frankly, I have never heard of anyone who has fulfilled a mere seven of these biblical requirements for the Messiah, yet Jesus fulfilled them all! Just as there is only one God to declare, there is only One Son of God who "declared Him"— meaning defined Him! For the loving and merciful God of the universe does not want anyone to go into eternity without faith in Jesus Christ as Creator, Savior, and King (see 2 Peter 3:9).

Throughout history, false Christs and false prophets have

deceived millions. During the Tribulation, many more will be deceived. And the extreme grief of Jesus seen at the end of Matthew chapter 23—when He lamented the Jewish people's rejection of Him—shows that the Jewish priests and religious leaders had deceived many as well. They had not adequately taught the messianic prophecies to the Jews in Jerusalem. Just days after large crowds had welcomed Jesus into the city as a great personage with miraculous powers, those same crowds either agreed with their religious leaders' rejection of Christ or remained silent while those leaders demanded He be killed by the Roman authorities.

The disciples also did not fully understand that Jesus was their nation's Messiah until after His bodily resurrection. Yet the three questions that they asked Him on the Mount of Olives indicated they were on the verge of belief. As the apostle Peter had already said, "Lord, to whom shall we go? You have the words of eternal life" (John 6:68).

One More End-Time Prophecy

In the course of answering the disciples' three questions, Jesus said this in reference to the last days: "You will hear of wars and rumors of wars. See that you are not troubled; for all these things must come to pass, but the end is not yet" Matthew 24:6

History has proven Jesus was right—the study of history is a study of war after war. My colleague of over 30 years, the late Dr. Henry M. Morris, the great creation scientist, wrote the following on this verse: "Worldwide, at least one major war has been going on in 11 out of every 12 years since the time of Christ. At the present time there are estimated to be at least 40 wars—small and large, civil or international—going on in the world."[1]

At the time of this writing, wars in the Middle East are exploding in and around Israel, Syria, and Iraq. There is also fighting going on in Russia, the Ukraine, and various parts of Africa, among other locations. We live in a time of continually increasing instability and warfare all across the globe. In fact, it is only a matter of time before the world will be plunged into another global war.

It's important to note that Jesus did not rebuke the disciples for asking the three questions they posed to Him: "When will these things be? And what shall be the sign of your coming, and of the end of the age?" (Matthew 24:3). He knew that for the next 2000 years, those would be the very questions that would concern many of His followers. They all have to do with the timing of His promised kingdom. They were asking, "When will You come back, and what sign can we expect of Your coming?" It's clear that they expected He would come back. They seemed to understand He was going to His Father's house, as He had predicted, and that would come back again as He promised (see John 14:1-3). And naturally, they wanted to know *when* this would happen. So do we!

In fact, my wife Beverly and I (Tim) ask a similar question. We've been married for 68 wonderful years. Our question is this: Will we be taken together in the rapture, or will we go to heaven separately?

The good news is that because of our faith in Jesus, no matter when it is that He comes, ultimately, we will be together in eternity forever. No wonder the apostle Paul was inspired to speak of "looking for the blessed hope and glorious appearing of our great God and Savior Jesus Christ" (Titus 2:13). That "hope" is not just a divine promise; it is a divine certainty that we can have confidence in, for it is the promise of God.

Jesus' Warning

While it is legitimate for Christians to enjoy this hope or divine confidence that Christ will return for His followers someday, no one knows the day or the hour of His coming (Matthew 24:36-44; 25:13). Many people have made the mistake of attempting to predict the date of Christ's coming, even though Scripture forbids them from doing so. Jesus made it clear that no one knows the time of His coming, so we shouldn't waste our time trying to guess when He will return. Rather, we should be ready all the time because Jesus could come at any time!

Do Not Be Troubled by the World's Turmoil

In Matthew 24:6, Jesus cautioned us to remember that even when there are wars and rumors of wars, we should not let our hearts be troubled. We should not let the news of such events unnerve us. Why? "For all these things must come to pass, but the end is not yet." That is, we should expect these things to happen. They must come to pass. And how do we keep our hearts from being troubled? By trusting in the Lord. He is faithful. He is in control. Rather than worry, we are to rest in Him.

The War Sign That Fits Jesus' Prophecy

It is interesting to observe the specifics Jesus included in His prophecy in Matthew 24:6-7. After mentioning "wars and rumors of wars," He says we should not be troubled because "the end is not yet." Then He says this: "Nation will rise against nation, and kingdom against kingdom. And there will be famines, pestilences, and earthquakes in various places" (verse 7). That is, there's more that would happen. Here's what they are:

1. A war started by two nations—until the whole world is involved

2. Famines

3. Pestilences (diseases)

4. Earthquakes in various places simultaneously

Jesus goes from talking about wars in general to a discussion about a certain kind of war that involves two nations who are joined by other nations until the whole world is involved, accompanied by three divinely inspired catastrophes. Could such a war accelerate into global proportions? All four elements of Matthew 24:7 were present in World War I, which took place from 1914 to 1918 and took the lives of an estimated 50 million people. That war began as a conflict between Serbia and Austria but drew in many other nations. Therefore, it is not difficult to see how a similar conflict could arise in the future and end up involving the whole globe.

The Climax of Jewish Hatred

Almost simultaneous with the rise of the Zionist movement was a growing and satanically inspired hatred toward the Hebrew people from Spain, Italy, Germany, Poland, Russia, and even England. This hatred led to breaking the Balfour Treaty, which individuals like General Gordon, Field Marshal Allenby, and Lord Belfour had used, along with their influence, to make it possible for the Jews to return to their homeland. It is unfortunate that the land of Israel ever came to be called *Palestine*, for the Bible repeatedly calls it the land of Israel. The name came into use by Rome after the Bar Kochba Revolt as an insult to the Jews. The Roman designation *Palestina* is the Latin name of the ancient Philistines, the Old Testament enemies of Israel. By the time of the Roman conquests in AD 70 and 135, the Philistines had been long gone. What's more, the Old Testament Philistines were not Arabs, nor were they related to Arabs. Unfortunately, the name *Palestine* has continued to be used on maps of the Middle East for the last several centuries, which has furthered the confusion people have today with regard to the origin of the term *Palestine*.

Target Israel

When Jesus answered the disciples' questions about the last days, He did so not to frighten them, but to comfort them. And He's not the only one who proclaimed Bible prophecy with that goal in mind. The apostle Paul did this as well. For example, in the Bible's most detailed passage about the rapture of the church, Paul wrote, "Comfort one another with these words" (1 Thessalonians 4:18). I

(Tim) have been a minister of the gospel for 68 years, and 37 of those years, I was a pastor. During that time, I have seen 1 Thessalonians 4:18 offer hope to many of God's people. Thousands of pastors have quoted this verse at the funerals of departed saints, reminding fellow believers of God's promise that we will one day be reunited in heaven.

Then in the very next chapter, Paul again points out—in the context of end-time prophecy—that this information is to be a source of comfort (1 Thessalonians 5:1-11). He concludes by saying, "Therefore encourage one another and build up one another, just as you also are doing" (verse 11). As Dr. Hindson has often said at our prophecy conferences, "God has not revealed these end-time truths to scare us but to prepare us for the Lord's return."

It is also noteworthy that both our Lord, in His greatest of all end-time prophecy instruction, the Olivet Discourse, and the apostle Paul made significant efforts to inform us so that we could understand the "times and seasons" of His return without knowing "the day or the hour." Even though date-setting or speculation on the *when* of Jesus' coming is forbidden, they forthrightly spoke about the end times to motivate Christians toward greater personal holiness and to communicate a sense of urgency about reaching the lost.

The Prophetic Birth Pains Have Already Begun

Just as an expectant mother's birth pains serve as a warning that she is about to deliver her child, Jesus spoke of prophetic birth pains that are "the beginning of sorrows" (Matthew 24:8). In this book we will show that the events that are blossoming into these prophetic birth pains have already begun or are well under way. For example, back in the nineteenth century secularist and humanist worldviews began to be taught in the universities of Europe and then America. Secularism and humanism have both fueled the anti-God sentiments that are so common in today's culture. They had their start in academic institutions, and have filtered into other areas of our lives.

One popular element of these worldviews is the idea of all nations and peoples moving toward a one-world government. And that's exactly what the Bible tells us will happen in the last days.

It is the birth pains taking place around us that make it clear we may well be living in the the last days spoken of by Jesus and His prophets. God alone can declare "the end from the beginning" (Isaiah 46:9-10)—that is, only He knows what will take place in the future. The fact many of the prophecies in the Bible have been fulfilled exactly as predicted is proof of God's omniscience and evidence that He exists. Bible prophecy is history written in advance, and only God can reveal with perfect certainty what is to come.

It is our contention that Israel's re-establishment as a nation— the valley of bones coming to life—is the greatest sign of our Lord's imminent return, which could be very close at hand. It is what we call the "super sign" of the last days.

CHAPTER 6

The Prophetic Promise of Jesus

Do you think, based on the chaos present in our world, that we are living in the most terrible time in history? The Lord Jesus Christ, the greatest prophet in the entire Bible, would say no. According to His Olivet Discourse, the worst is yet to come. In Matthew 24:21, He said, "Then there will be great tribulation, such as has not been since the beginning of the world until this time, no, nor ever shall be." These words introduce the second half of the Tribulation, when the Antichrist will take complete control of this world.

Things will get so bad that God, in His mercy, will shorten that time of destruction. Matthew 24:22 says that "for the elect's sake those days will be shortened." In Revelation chapters 6–20 we find that God will so shake the earth and all its natural forces that millions of undecided people will turn to Christ. During the Tribulation, God, His Son Jesus Christ, and the Holy Spirit will be in a titanic battle against Satan, his demon spirits, and the false prophet for the souls of the undecided. God, in His great love and mercy for humanity, will send 144,000 Jewish witnesses, the two supernatural witnesses of Revelation 11, and do other things to convict people of their sins and their need to call upon the Lord to receive the gift of eternal salvation.

A thorough reading of the book of Revelation reveals the many expressions of God's great love for mankind even during that short seven-year period that will precede the end of the world. Satan will know his time is short and will do everything he can to deceive mankind about God and the Savior, as he has done ever since the Garden of Eden. One of the many expressions of God's love and mercy will be the three angels in Revelation 14. Note what the apostle John said about one of these angels: One of those angels will "fly in the midst of heaven, having the everlasting gospel to preach to those who dwell on the earth." Revelation 14:6-7 notes:

> I saw another angel flying in the midst of heaven, having the everlasting gospel to preach to those who dwell on the earth—to every nation, tribe, tongue, and people— saying with a loud voice, "Fear God and give glory to Him, for the hour of His judgment has come; and worship Him who made heaven and earth, the sea and springs of water."

A detailed study of Revelation reveals at least 39 events that will show God's great love and mercy during the Apocalypse. That should not surprise us. God will act as He always has, showing His love (John 3:16) and His yearning will for all people (2 Peter 3:9). In the Old Testament, God described Himself personally to Moses as one who is "merciful and gracious, longsuffering, and abounding in goodness and truth, keeping mercy for thousands, forgiving iniquity and transgression and sin (Exodus 24:6-7). Second Peter 3:9 tells us of God's great patience toward sinners: "The Lord is not slack concerning His promise, as some count slackness, but is longsuffering toward us, not willing that any should perish but that all should come to repentance." And this love will be made known "to every nation, tribe, tongue, and people" even during the Tribulation

(Revelation 14:6). saying with a loud voice, "Fear [meaning revere] God."

What's more, in John chapter 5, after Jesus gave the unbelieving Jews of His day some incredible reasons for believing He was the one and only Messiah of God, He put the blame for their unbelief on them, not on God. He said, "You are not willing to come to Me that you may have life."

It is a matter of will. Jesus Himself said, "If anyone wills to do His will, he shall know concerning the doctrine, whether it is from God or whether I speak on My own authority" (John 7:17). If a person is willing to do God's will, "he shall know concerning the doctrine" or the teaching about Himself. The Savior who, during the Tribulation, will send an angel from heaven to reach the lost, or who sent Peter to the home of a sincere pagan centurion named Cornelius in Acts 10, or who sent a missionary evangelist I know to a tribe of headhunters, is abundantly able to send a messenger or the gospel message to anyone who sincerely seeks God.

If a theologian's view of the God of the Bible includes the inexhaustible extent of His sovereign knowledge, he should have little difficulty accepting the fact that when any person makes the decision to accept or reject His Son, Jesus, that God the Father is never taken by surprise. He knew, before the foundation of the world, who would receive Christ and who would reject Him. Those who choose not to accept Jesus Christ will be cast into the Lake of Fire (Revelation 20:15). This fire was never designed for mankind, but for the devil and his angels. The choice of every man or woman to accept Christ is his or hers alone. God will never force you to accept His Son.

The Key to Understanding the Olivet Discourse

As we noted earlier, just days before Jesus' death and resurrection, the disciples asked Him three questions about His future kingdom and the signs of His coming. That these questions are important to us as well is evident in the fact that Jesus gave not just three, but at least nine or more answers in the verses that follow. Some of the answers He provided could be divided into additional responses.

There are, however, three answers that stand out because together, they make it clear that the prophecies in Matthew 24–25 have not all been fulfilled. They are as follows:

- a world war started by two small nations
- the gospel being taught around the entire world (as described in Revelation 14)
- the desecration of the temple in the last days

We've already looked in some detail at the first two items. As for the desecration of the temple, that has not yet happened. It won't occur until the Antichrist makes a seven-year covenant or treaty with the Jews, for it is at the midpoint of that treaty (three-and-a-half years into the Tribulation) that the desecration will take place (see Daniel 9:27; 11:31; 2 Thessalonians 2:3-4; Revelation 13:5). This seven-year treaty won't take place until after the rapture of the church. However, this could all come together in a very short time. The rapture is the next event on God's prophetic calendar, which means it could happen at any time. And even though there is no temple in Jerusalem at the present, that could change quickly if the "man of sin," known as the Antichrist, allows for it to be rebuilt, for he is the one who will desecrate it (2 Thessalonians 2:3-4).

This desecration of the temple is also known as the "abomination of desolation" (Matthew 24:15; see also Daniel 11:31). Unfortunately for the Jews, it is at this point that the Antichrist, who confirmed a seven-year peace treaty with them, will turn on them. He will defile the temple, and this won't be the first time that has happened. This occurred once before when the evil Antiochus Epiphanes, a Syrian king who ruled the region from 175–165 BC, sacrificed a pig on the altar in the temple. It is noteworthy here to point out that Jesus, in

Matthew 24:15, acknowledged Daniel as the official author of the book of Daniel. This stands in contrast to the view of liberal scholars who claim Daniel did not write the book that bears his name.

In Matthew 24:15, Jesus gave His disciples and us a clear and unmistakable sign of both the Tribulation and the Antichrist: "When you see the 'abomination of desolation,' spoken of by Daniel the prophet, standing in the holy place…" When the Antichrist appears on the scene, he will make as part of his covenant with the Jews an agreement to let them rebuild their temple in Jerusalem during the first half of the Tribulation. However, at the midpoint of the Tribulation, after he has united the world under one government, he will break his covenant with the Jews and declare himself God. Second Thessalonians 2:3-4 gives us the details:

> That Day will not come unless the falling away comes
> first, and the man of sin is revealed, the son of perdition,
> who opposes and exalts himself above all that is called
> God or that is worshiped, so that he sits as God in the
> temple of God, showing himself that he is God.

At this time the Antichrist will deceive many unbelievers into worshipping him as God, giving what Satan has wanted since the Garden of Eden—to be worshipped.

This abomination of desolation is coming. After the rapture of the church, half of the judgments of the Tribulation planned by God to bring millions of people to faith in Christ will take place. Daniel 9 speaks of these events in detail. More specifically, we are told this in Daniel 9:2, after the Persians had conquered the Babylonians: "In the first year of his reign I, Daniel, understood by the books the number of the years specified by the word of the LORD through Jeremiah the prophet, that He would accomplish seventy years in the desolations of Jerusalem." At this point Daniel began to pray, confessing his sins and the sins of the nation of Israel. Then the Lord sent the angel Gabriel with a special message for Daniel, which according to verses 22-23, is to give Daniel the "skill to understand...the vision." Here is the vision given to Daniel:

> Seventy weeks are determined
> For your people and for your holy city,
> To finish the transgression,
> To make an end of sins,
> To make reconciliation for iniquity,
> To bring in everlasting righteousness,
> To seal up vision and prophecy,
> And to anoint the Most Holy.
>
> Know therefore and understand,
> That from the going forth of the command
> To restore and build Jerusalem
> Until Messiah the Prince,
> There shall be seven weeks and sixty-two weeks;
> The street shall be built again, and the wall,
> Even in troublesome times.
>
> And after the sixty-two weeks
> Messiah shall be cut off, but not for Himself;
> And the people of the prince who is to come
> Shall destroy the city and the sanctuary.
> The end of it shall be with a flood,
> And till the end of the war desolations are determined.
> Then he shall confirm a covenant with many for one week;
> But in the middle of the week
> He shall bring an end to sacrifice and offering.
> And on the wing of abominations shall be one who
>   makes desolate,
> Even until the consummation, which is determined,
> Is poured out on the desolate (verses 24-27).

It is most important to understand the time period involved here. The Hebrew term translated "seven" refers to a unit of seven rather than seven days, and only the context reveals how much time is involved. The word should literally be translated "sevens" or "heptads" ("group of seven"). We have a similar expression in English. For example, if I say a dozen, I could mean a dozen weeks or a dozen years. The same is true of this Hebrew word.

If we study the context, it is clear from both Daniel and Revelation 12 that these sevens are weeks of years or heptads of years. Daniel's 70 weeks are literally 70 units of 7 years, or 490 years. These 490 years are divided into three groups that must be understood in order to comprehend the time element, as featured on the accompanying chart.

Seven sevens of years equals 49 years. A study of Jewish history reveals that from the going forth of the decree of Cyrus, it took the Jews under both Ezra and Nehemiah 49 years to complete the building of the walls of the city of Jerusalem. This first unit, or time of restoration (verse 25), was fulfilled as predicted.

Sixty-two sevens (or "weeks" in some translations) of years equals 434 years. These next 434 years, described as 62 weeks or heptads, were predicted to be "times of trouble," a very accurate description of this period. It was a time of silence from God until John the Baptist began his ministry. It was a time of weakness in Israel. This period was predicted to end when the "Messiah shall be cut off, but not for Himself." This second period, extending from the rebuilding of the temple to the crucifixion of Christ, equals a total of 434 years.

Since all the prophecies regarding Christ's first coming were fulfilled without any deviation, we can well assume the precise fulfillment of this one. Sir Robert Anderson's masterful book, *The Coming Prince*, shows that Christ's arrival into Jerusalem the Sunday before His crucifixion occurred in exactly the right year. To my (Tim's) knowledge, his book has never been refuted.

One week equals seven years. Daniel 9:27 predicts that the Antichrist will make a covenant with Israel for one "week." No one has made such a covenant with Israel since the time of Christ's crucifixion. So we know this event is still in the future.

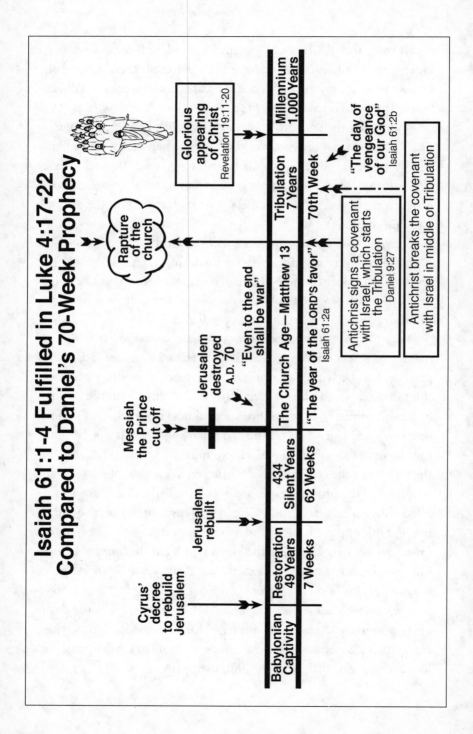

Isaiah 61:1-4 Fulfilled in Luke 4:17-22 Compared to Daniel's 70-Week Prophecy

Cyrus' decree to rebuild Jerusalem

Jerusalem rebuilt

Messiah the Prince cut off

Jerusalem destroyed A.D. 70

"Even to the end shall be war"

Rapture of the church

Glorious appearing of Christ
Revelation 19:11-20

| Babylonian Captivity | Restoration 49 Years | 434 Silent Years | The Church Age—Matthew 13 | Tribulation 7 Years | Millennium 1,000 Years |

7 Weeks — 62 Weeks — 70th Week

"The year of the LORD's favor"
Isaiah 61:2a

"The day of vengeance of our God"
Isaiah 61:2b

Antichrist signs a covenant with Israel, which starts the Tribulation
Daniel 9:27

Antichrist breaks the covenant with Israel in middle of Tribulation

When the Antichrist breaks his covenant with Israel in the middle of the seven-year Tribulation, things will still be within the period of time that the angel Gabriel predicted would be "determined for your people and for your holy city" (Daniel 9:24). The first two divisions of these 70 units of years total 483 years. All but one "week," or heptad, of Israel's prophetically determined history has been accomplished. This final week will be such that the people of God are referred to as "the desolate" (verse 27). The latter part of Daniel 9:26 indicates that there will be a time of interruption in this prophetic calendar: "And till the end of the war desolations are determined." This corresponds with Isaiah's reference to "the acceptable year of the Lord" (Isaiah 61:2), which is the Christian dispensation—the year of God's grace to the Gentiles. This will culminate in Isaiah 61:2 with "the day of vengeance of our God," which is the resumption of God's prophetic calendar for Israel, or the seventieth week of Daniel or the Tribulation period.

This will be followed by the second phase of Christ's coming to the earth, which the apostle Paul calls the "glorious appearing" (Titus 2:13). When will this occur?

> Immediately after the tribulation of those days the sun will be darkened, and the moon will not give its light; the stars will fall from heaven, and the powers of the heavens will be shaken. Then the sign of the Son of Man will appear in heaven, and then all the tribes of the earth will mourn, and they will see the Son of Man coming on the clouds of heaven with power and great glory (Matthew 24:29-30).

We will discuss this glorious appearing in more detail in a later chapter. For now, we're going to look next at Scripture's symbolic reference to Israel as a fig tree—a matter of significance for both the nation of Israel and Christians today.

CHAPTER 7

Israel as a Fig Tree

When we attempt to understand God's Word, it's dangerous to automatically assume a spiritual or symbolic meaning for what is being said. It is better to follow the basic rule taught by David L. Cooper, who taught the Golden Rule of Bible Interpretation: "When the plain sense of Scripture makes common sense, seek no other sense; therefore, take every word at its primary, ordinary, usual, literal meaning unless the facts of the immediate context...indicate clearly otherwise."[1]

The chiliastic doctrine of the early church of the first three centuries taught that Christ would come premillennially—that is, before He was to establish the millennial kingdom, which is why they received the title *chiliasts* or premillennialists.

Amillennialism, which spiritualizes or allegorizes Scripture, particularly the prophetic passages, eventually supplanted the views of the earliest church fathers. This trend increased rapidly in the fourth and fifth centuries, with Augustine changing the popular view of prophecy to amillennialism. This teaching views the present church age as the kingdom of God on earth. Details about the prophetic future are generally limited to a final judgment and the eternal state. Amillennialists see no particular prophetic significance for Israel and generally believe that the church is the new "Israel." The problem, however, with not taking the plain meaning of Scripture literally is that it opens the door to redefining God's Word to mean almost anything.

Those who spiritualize the approximately 28 percent of the Bible that is prophetic have come up with interpretations that have adversely affected even the basic doctrines of the church. Thankfully, one of the things that has helped to offset that is the passion that God placed in the hearts of people like John Wycliffe and William Tyndale to translate the Bible into the languages of the common people of Europe in the fourteenth and fifteenth centuries. It was during this same era that Johann Gutenberg developed the first movable-type printing press in Europe, making it much easier to produce books in quantity. Among the books he printed was the Gutenberg Bible. All this spurred a move toward Bibles translated and written for the common people, who could at last read the Word of God for themselves. When they did so, they took it literally, believing God said what He meant and meant what He said. As time went on, this eventually contributed to the study of Bible prophecy, the resurgence of evangelism, and a return to the belief that Christ would come to rapture the church before the Tribulation and the end of the age.

The Bible continues to be read by countless people worldwide. In fact, it is the most popular book in the world. Books that have sold a million copies are widely acclaimed. But only the Bible has over 35 *billion* copies in print. Which is why it does not appear on the *New York Times* bestseller list. It wins every year!

In addition, Christianity has the largest number of followers in the world. The Christian worldview says, "In the beginning God created the heavens and the earth" (Genesis 1:1). By contrast, the secular or godless worldview says, "Man is the measure of all things." Ultimately, a God-centered view of life leads to eternity with God through the gift of His only Son, whereas the secular or godless view of life leads to eternity without God.

Interestingly enough, ever since the spread of the Bible in the languages of the common people, the church has largely returned to the premillennial view of the end times as held by the early church of the first three centuries. But there are still some today who tend to spiritualize the 28 percent of the Bible that is prophetic and have embraced amillennialism, or the idea that we are now living in the millennium and that the church has replaced Israel in end-times prophecy (also called Replacement Theology). This view says that Christians do not need to see the prophecies related to Israel as literally being fulfilled by Israel and the Jewish people. Thus they can ignore God's promises pertaining to Israel's place in the land.

That is why many people today are willing to abandon Israel on the present world scene. But if we who are in America don't obey our Lord's command to "learn the parable from the fig tree" (Matthew 24:32) and bless Israel, we could lose God's protective hand upon our nation and incur His wrath as He deals with the decadence and moral depravity that are so rampant in our midst. For these reasons we urge Christians to pray for a moral and spiritual revival in America and to continue doing good to the nation of Israel. This is what is needed to save our own nation and guarantee its future blessing.

The Significance of the Fig Tree

With that in mind, let's turn our attention to learning from the parable of the fig tree as it relates to God's plans for Israel (and for our nation!). In this parable we are instructed to take Israel as a prophetic picture of end-time prophecy. Jesus said, "Now learn this parable from the fig tree: When its branch has already become tender and puts forth leaves, you know that summer is near" (Matthew 24:32).

This parable speaks of a very specific sign of the end times—the sign of Jesus' coming back to earth to establish His kingdom. He brings this up in response to the disciples' question, "What will be the sign of your coming?" (verse 3). Notice He made no mention of the rapture of the church. The church did not begin until a little over 40 days later, when the Holy Spirit descended upon the disciples, representing Himself and God the Father and the Son in one accord (Acts 2:1-47). The signs Jesus referred to had to do with His literal return to the earth to reign in the millennium.

It is important to note here that the early church was founded in full view of large crowds in the city of Jerusalem. So when Peter said, "We did not follow cunningly devised fables when we made known to you the power and coming of our Lord Jesus Christ, but were eyewitnesses of His majesty" (1 Peter 1:16), no one could refute him. That's because he, the other disciples, and at least 3000 new converts were witnesses to all that took place at the birth of the church, at which time they testified to the miracles of Jesus coming as Messiah and the supreme sacrifice for our sins. Talk about credibility! That is tremendous evidence for the truthfulness of the gospel story regarding the death, burial, and resurrection—evidence that would stand up in any objective court in the world.

Returning to the account of the fig tree, our Lord intended for this parable to serve as an illustration. What is a parable? One simple definition given by Bible teachers is that a parable is an earthly story with a heavenly meaning. That is how at least three Hebrew prophets—Hosea, Joel, and Jeremiah—spoke of fig trees in the Old Testament. They used the fig tree as a symbol of Israel, a symbol that forecast God's future dealings with the nation. Let's take a look at what each of these prophets said.

In the Old Testament
Hosea, the Prophet of God's Everlasting Love for Israel

Hosea is the first of the minor prophets in the Old Testament (circa 755–710 BC). He prophesied about God's undying love for Israel and was also the first writer in the Old Testament to mention the fig tree as a symbol of Israel. His ministry took place during one of the lowest times in Israel's history—when the ten tribes of the northern kingdom, due to their wickedness and depravity, were taken away into captivity in 722 BC by the Assyrians.

Hosea's assignment may have also been one of the most unusual of any prophet. In Hebrews 13:4, God made it clear that the marriage bed is to be "undefiled." Yet God commanded Hosea to marry a prostitute, have children with her, and then forgive her when she was unfaithful and buy her back from slavery. We may find it unthinkable that God would ask Hosea to do this. Yet it illustrates that the God Hosea served was a forgiving God. Even in the face of Israel's flagrant sins and unfaithfulness to God, forgiveness was available if the people would repent and return to Him. Unfortunately, they refused God's warning of judgment and were taken into slavery by the Assyrians and scattered—just as God predicted.

There are many lessons that can be learned from Hosea's account. But of particular interest to us is Hosea 9:10, where God says, "I have found Israel…as the firstfruits on the fig tree."

Joel, the Prophet of the End Times

Joel referred to the end times as "the day of the LORD" (Joel 2:1). This could refer to an imminent time when a person or nation must give account of himself or itself to God. It can also be used in reference to an ultimate future time of divine judgment by God. In general, it is a term that can be applied to past, present, or future events, depending on the context. That is why prophecy must be studied carefully, so that one can determine which period of time the "day of the LORD" refers to. For God holds people responsible for their behavior—how faithful are they about the way they use their talents, time, influence, and resources?

Joel lived more than 100 years before Isaiah. He ministered in Israel during a period when the nation had departed from obeying the Lord. Joel's warnings and prophecies in Joel 1:4-6 spoke of God's impending judgment in the form of a massive plague of locusts that would devour the land's crops. Joel then called to the elders of the nation for a spiritual revival. Evidently the two tribes of the southern kingdom responded enough to allow them to escape the judgment faced by the ten northern tribes that were scattered by the Assyrians.

Then Joel directly addressed the two southern tribes on behalf of God, saying, "He has laid waste My vine, and ruined My fig tree; He has stripped it bare and thrown it away; its branches are made white" (Joel 1:7). Again, we see the Lord using the fig tree as a symbol of Israel.

Jeremiah, the Great Unappreciated Prophet

Jeremiah, who is popularly known as "the suffering prophet," began his lengthy 55-year ministry in 627 BC. The king for much of that time was Josiah, a good king. Because Isaiah prophesied that Jerusalem would be destroyed because of the people's sins and rejection of God, he was persecuted by his own countrymen. Though Jeremiah was a contemporary of Daniel and Ezekiel, who were taken captive to Babylon, they probably never met, for Jeremiah lived most of his life in Jerusalem, and his last days were spent in Egypt, where he was taken against his will.

Of all the Old Testament prophets, Jeremiah prophesied more about the Messiah than any other. He spoke of Jesus coming as a human to die as God's special sacrifice for mankind. He also predicted the second coming of Christ in power in the last days to rule over the future kingdom age. The fact that Jeremiah's prophecies about Christ's first appearance were fulfilled serves as a guaranteeing that his end-time prophecies will also be fulfilled.

Now let's look at what Jeremiah said about the fig tree as a symbol of the southern two kingdoms of Israel:

> The Lord showed me, and there were two baskets of figs set before the temple of the Lord, after Nebuchadnezzar king of Babylon had carried away captive Jeconiah the son of Jehoiakim, king of Judah, and the princes of

Judah with the craftsmen and smiths, from Jerusalem, and had brought them to Babylon. One basket had very good figs, like the figs that are first ripe; and the other basket had very bad figs which could not be eaten, they were so bad. Then the LORD said to me, "What do you see, Jeremiah?"

And I said, "Figs, the good figs, very good; and the bad, very bad, which cannot be eaten, they are so bad."

Again the word of the LORD came to me, saying, "Thus says the LORD, the God of Israel: 'Like these good figs, so will I acknowledge those who are carried away captive from Judah, whom I have sent out of this place for their own good, into the land of the Chaldeans. For I will set My eyes on them for good, and I will bring them back to this land; I will build them and not pull them down, and I will plant them and not pluck them up. Then I will give them a heart to know Me, that I am the LORD; and they shall be My people, and I will be their God, for they shall return to Me with their whole heart.

'And as the bad figs which cannot be eaten, they are so bad'—surely thus says the LORD—'so will I give up Zedekiah the king of Judah, his princes, the residue of Jerusalem who remain in this land, and those who dwell in the land of Egypt'" (Jeremiah 24:1-8).

Then in verses 9-10, Jeremiah goes on to say this:

I will deliver them to trouble into all the kingdoms of the earth, for their harm, to be a reproach and a byword, a taunt and a curse, in all places where I shall drive them. And I will send the sword, the famine, and the pestilence among them, till they are consumed from the land that I gave to them and their fathers.

This is similar to Jesus' own prophecy about the Jewish nation in

His Olivet Discourse. The people would be scattered, but there is coming a time when they will return. And as Jesus said in Matthew 24:32, "Now learn this parable from the fig tree: When its branch has already become tender and puts forth leaves, you know that summer is near" (Matthew 24:32). Comparing these scriptures with each other, we see evidence to believe Israel today is being brought back into the Holy Land as a sovereign state in these troubled times. This clearly indicates we are living in the "season" of the last days, or as we like to call it, "the last days of the last days."

Jesus Christ performed miracles during His ministry that produced positive results. He restored sight to blind eyes, hearing to those born deaf, and healed all manner of diseases, even curing ten lepers at one time. All these miracles proved He possessed the power of Almighty God.

Only once did He use that divine power to perform a miracle with negative results—when He came to a fig tree expecting it to refresh Him with some figs, which was customary in that day, and found that it had no fruit to offer. He cursed the fig tree, not in anger, but to teach a lesson to the disciples: When trees are in bloom (during the spring), it's an indication that the season for bearing fruit is drawing close (in the summer). Likewise, when we see the signs of Christ's coming, we can know His return is near. As Jesus Himself said, "When you see all these things, know that it is near—at the doors!" (Matthew 24:33).

CHAPTER 8

The Miracle of Israel's Regathering

Everything about Israel and the Jewish people is miraculous. Consider the nation's supernatural origin: It all started when a 90-year old woman was impregnated by a 99-year old man after they were no longer capable of bearing children. And the nation still exists after 4000 years while other nations and peoples have become extinct. Through the centuries, entire nations and governments have either rejected them or attempted to wipe them out. Today the Jewish people number around 14 million people in spite of consistent satanic hatred and efforts to destroy them.

During my last year of Air Force duty in Germany immediately after World War II, I (Tim) got the distinct impression that under Hitler, many Germans had been persuaded by the notion they were really a superior race of people in comparison to the Jews. It was such thinking that led to the horrors of the Holocaust. Forgive me if I sound harsh, but I have never forgotten my visit to the Dachau prison camp shortly after Germany surrendered to the Allied Forces. The smell of death still permeated the air, and it was heartbreaking to think of the countless deaths that took place in the gas chambers there.

Fortunately, for the sake of history, our supreme commander of the Allied Forces, General Dwight D. Eisenhower, promptly issued orders that many photographs be taken of our troops freeing the Jews who had been in the Nazi prison camps. Those photos stand as irrefutable evidence in the face of deniers who reject the fact that the Holocaust ever took place. Yet the denials not only persist; they are increasing in number! Many World War II veterans, myself included, can testify to the fact of the naked, starving, and emaciated bodies that inhabited those camps. That's forever etched into our memories. In addition, we remember the elated expressions on the faces of the Jewish prisoners when they realized the military personnel who came into their prisons were not Gestapo troops coming to gas them to death, but rather American and Allied soldiers coming to rescue them and give them liberty and victory.

I believe that our country's role in helping to free the Jewish people at the end of World War II is one of the reasons God has blessed America, in fulfillment of His divine promise in Genesis 12:1-3—a promise that has never been revoked! There are many other acts of mercy and care we have shown as well. Though we have not always been perfect in our treatment of the Jewish people, they have received more mercy and blessing from America than from any other country in the world. It is our prayer that this may never change—not just so we can continue to receive God's blessings, but because it is the right thing to do. As God said, He will bless those who bless Israel, and curse those who curse Israel.

While the world's hatred toward Israel manifests itself in many different ways, ultimately, it all has its origins in the work of Satan. Remember what happened after Jesus' birth? King Herod commanded that all the male children in Bethlehem who were two years old and younger be killed (Matthew 2:16). Satan inspired this plot in the hopes of derailing God's plan for Jesus to die on the cross to make salvation possible for all mankind. Repeatedly through the ages, Satan has attempted to thwart God's plans, and the mere fact Israel exists today as a nation is affirmation that God's plan is still on track—a fact that displeases Satan to no end.

So when we see anti-Semitism today—the kind that inspires the Arab nations to wipe Israel out or that causes European nations to look the other way when Jewish people are persecuted—we can be sure Satan is behind it all.

A Rabbi's Amazing 1800-Year Weather Phenomenon

Rabbi Menachem Kohen, a scholar of both the Old Testament prophecies and the additional prophecies of the Oral Torah, also carefully preserved through the ages, wrote an amazing book titled *Prophecies for the Era of Muslim Terror*, which was published in 2000. In the book he talks about how, after the Roman army destroyed Jerusalem and the temple, the Jews were expelled from most of the Holy Land and scattered throughout the world.

The rabbi then states that the Jewish people have experienced two miraculous returns to the land—the first one taking place after the Babylonian captivity (a dispersal predicted in Deuteronomy 28:38,63-64), and the second one taking place throughout the twentieth century and into today, some 1800 years after being scattered all around the world. In the latter case, just a small number of Jews remained in the land, which was called Palestine to spite the Jews. The land that had once been flowing with milk and honey became a desert for lack of rainfall for a little under two millennia, or as the rabbi said, for 660,000 days. By this he meant a period of more than 1800 years. Even the famous author Mark Twain, who visited the Holy Land in 1867, gave this appraisal of it: "The Israeli soil is rich enough but is wholly given to weeds...only desolation here...Jerusalem is lifeless. I would not desire to live there."[1]

The miracle here is that the timing puts the start of limited rainfall in the land of Palestine in the same century as the beginning of the Jewish migration back into the land. Ever so slowly, the displaced Jews around the world have felt, in their hearts, a desire to go back, and their numbers have increased in recent decades. Their return fulfills God's prophecy in Amos 9:14-15: "I will bring back the captives of My people Israel…I will plant them in their land, and no longer shall they be pulled up from the land I have given them."

The Highlights of Israel's Return

Our late colleague and friend Dr. James Combs was among the four Bible scholars who helped to produce the *LaHaye Prophecy Study Bible*. His article, "Israel in Two Centuries," was about that very period:

> The restoration of Israel, leading to a golden age of blessing, is a prominent theme in Scripture. No passage more graphically illustrates the process than Ezekiel 37.
>
> This vision of the dry bones as the "whole house of Israel" has five stages: 1) the dry bones are scattered around (v. 2); 2) the bones come together, develop connective tissues, and are covered with flesh (vv. 7-8); 3) the wind blows breath into these bodies (vv. 9-10); 4) the restoration is also a spiritual one (vv. 24-28); and 5) "David," actually Jesus Christ, the "Root and the Offspring of David" (Rev. 22:16), will reign over the nation.[2]

Setting no dates for specific fulfillments but surveying the trend of Israel's resurgence in the nineteenth and twentieth centuries, it appears this divine program of restoration is in progress. Dr. Combs points out the following highlights from these two centuries:

> 1814—Presbyterian pastor John MacDonald in Albany, New York, began to preach on Bible prophecy and Israel's restoration, sparking an interest in the literalist interpretation of Old Testament prophecies about Israel.

1878—W.E. Blackstone's book *Jesus Is Coming* was published, predicting and encouraging the return of Jews in fulfillment of the prophecy.

1881–1900—The First Aliya (meaning ascent [or return]) occurred and consisted of some 30,000 Jews under persecution in Russia moving to Palestine.

1897—The First Zionist Congress, convened in Basel, Switzerland, adopted Zionism as a program, and stated, "The aim of Zionism is to create for the Jewish people a home in Palestine by public law."

1904–1914—The Second Aliya resulted in 32,000 persecuted Russian Jews moving to Palestine.

1917—The Balfour Declaration read in part: "His majesty's government views with favor the establishment in Palestine of a national home for Jewish people."

1924–1939—The Third Aliya, when 78,000 Polish Jews moved to Palestine.

1933–1939—The Fourth Aliya, when 230,000 Jews fled from persecution in Germany and central Europe.

1940–1948—The Fifth Aliya, when 95,000 Jews escaped from central Europe. Many Jews remained in Europe, and more than six million were killed during the Holocaust led by Adolph Hitler and Nazi Germany.

1948—The Jewish Agency, in what would become the new nation of Israel, proclaimed nation status. On May 14, 1948, the United States President Harry Truman's administration made this announcement: "The United States recognizes the provisional government as the de facto authority of the New State of Israel."

1967—The Six-Day War, precipitated by an Arab invasion, resulted in Israel capturing Jerusalem and the West Bank.

1973—Another attack by Arabs was repulsed with Israeli victories [in what is now known as the Yom Kippur War].

1978–2000—Egypt recognizes Israel; the Arab-Palestinian resistance movement began; negotiations, agreements, and tensions continue.[3]

At the time of this writing, the final item in this list by Dr. Combs is still ongoing.

It seems that during this time span, the dry bones have come together to form a living nation, one of the most powerful small nations on earth. But there awaits the complete spiritual awakening, when true life enters the people, as prophesied in Ezekiel 37.

Intervention on Israel's Behalf

A key date relating to Israel's migration back into the Promised Land is May 14, 1948, when President Harry Truman signed a letter that officially recognized the new State of Israel and its government. What is little known about President Truman is that he had been raised in a Christian home. As a young man he was an avid reader, and he said he had read the Bible twice by the time he was 12 years old.

It was an act of divine providence that God showed His blessing on Israel and the United States by making it possible for this obscure senator from Missouri to eventually become president and wield the influence that he did. When Franklin D. Roosevelt decided he would make an unprecedented run for a fourth term, he planned for his then-vice president Henry Wallace to stay on as his vice presidential candidate. However, a number of influential Democratic party members didn't want Wallace to stay on the ticket, and through a lot of political wrangling, managed to get Truman nominated in place of Wallace. When the nation voted in November 1944, Roosevelt and Truman were elected. Three months later Roosevelt died, and suddenly Harry Truman was catapulted into the presidency of the United States.

President Truman was not the only president to lead the US to reach out and help Israel when it was attacked by hostile enemies. In 1973, several Arab enemies launched a surprise attack on Israel on their high holy day of Yom Kippur. Because many Israeli military officers and men were at home on leave at the time, the nation was nearly defenseless at first. Initially Israel suffered great losses, but President Nixon worked quickly to rush aid to the country. He dispatched emergency airlifts of supplies and arms. Eventually Israel was able to push back, and once again God delivered Israel from an Arab coalition that wanted to drive the Jews into the sea. We believe that God sent His blessings upon America as a result of its support at this crucial time.

With regard to Nixon, it is alleged that his mother, who read the Bible, told him that one day he would have the opportunity to do something to help the Jewish people.

Friend or Foe of Israel?

It's amazing to see how God brings blessings upon people based on a nation's support of Israel.

One example of this occurred in our church during the early 1970s, at which time the United States had helped Israel during the Yom Kippur War. The church I (Tim) pastored in San Diego was growing rapidly, and we had to hold three morning services and two evening services to accommodate the crowds. A young engineer who attended our church, Al Mills, invited a colleague from his workplace to hear me preach on the miraculous ways that God was fulfilling Bible prophecies in our time. He came to two or three services and concluded we were crazy in spite of his admiration for his coworker.

Shortly afterward, he made a job-related move to the East Coast—right when the Arab nations attacked Israel. The media had predicted the battles would be fatal to Israel because the small nation was so outmatched. As it so happened—and I believe this was God's providence—that young skeptic became ill and was confined to his home when all the news stations were covering this attack. Things didn't look good for Israel—it didn't look like there was any chance of survival.

But what at first appeared to be the certain annihilation of Israel turned into supernatural preservation. This young man was a former naval officer, and what he saw on TV convinced him that there is indeed a God in heaven who is watching out for Israel. And he also became convicted of the gospel message that he had heard at our church—the message of why Jesus came to earth, and that God accepted His Son's sacrifice for sin so that people could be saved. Consequently, this man accepted Christ as His Savior by inviting Him into his heart.

A few days later I received a great letter from this man, thanking me for faithfully teaching about God and His plan of salvation. He said he had called on the name of the Lord to be saved. Many of us who had been praying for him rejoiced, and we look forward to seeing him one day in heaven.

We believe this is the kind of blessing God brings upon a nation that blesses Israel.

By contrast, Great Britain turned its back on Israel and reneged on its agreement to help the Jewish people establish a homeland. When it came time to divide up land that had formerly belonged to the Ottoman Empire, for a number of reasons, larger portions of that land were given to Arab entities. Ultimately, Britain capitulated to Arab demands regarding how the land was divided.

It was at this time that Britain's territorial influence was at its greatest. You may have heard the popular saying, "The sun never sets on the British Empire." At one time, that was true. But after Britain favored the Arabs over Israel, the British Empire began to decline, and it's been declining since. One cannot help but wonder if this is related to Britain's betrayal of Israel. The nation had chosen to side with Israel's enemies, and for that there is no divine promise of blessing. As God said in Genesis 12:3, "I will bless those who bless you, and I will curse him who curses you."

We believe that the spiritual, moral, and economic decline of Great Britain is largely due to the influence of secularists who exert a lot of control over the educational system, state church, and media. And the government has failed to stand up for Israel when there were opportunities to do so—thereby rejecting God's blessing upon their nation. We pray that the United States will not follow in these footsteps. If it does, then in light of God's promise in Genesis 12:3, we can expect to see a drastic decline in the quality of life in America.

A Key Time Indicator

Our Lord prophesied, "Now learn this parable from the fig tree: When its branch has already become tender and puts forth leaves, you know that summer is near" (Matthew 24:32). The tiny nation of Israel—the divinely selected "fig tree symbol"—has been gradually populated by Jewish people from all over the world. This means we are very close to the end times, as predicted by both Old and New Testament prophets, as well as by Jesus Christ in His Olivet Discourse. What's more, for the first time ever, mankind finds itself in the position of having the capability of destroying itself from the face of the earth, along with all of humanity. But that will not happen. How do we know? First, Jesus has not yet returned to rapture His church to heaven (1 Thessalonians 4:13-18). Second, the world has yet to go through the seven-year Tribulation (Revelation chapters 4–19). And after that, Jesus will set up His 1000-year millennial kingdom of peace on earth. The most evil-inspired terrorists or dictators will not pull the trigger for human destruction; God will not allow it. He alone declares "the end from the beginning" (Isaiah 46:10).

The fact that mankind is capable of destroying himself should not cause us to be fearful. Rather, it should cause us to have a concern for the lost. We have no idea how much time is left before the Lord takes us home in the rapture. As he said in John 14:1-3,

> Let not your heart be troubled; you believe in God, believe also in Me. In My Father's house are many mansions; if it were not so, I would have told you. I go to prepare a place for you. And if I go and prepare a place for you, I will come again and receive you to Myself; that where I am, there you may be also.

These verses highlight the fact that we should be prepared at any time to respond to the majestic rapture call of Jesus Christ. He is after all, the Creator, God of heaven and earth, and everything He does is done in His perfect timing.

Haggai Precedent

When God brought the people of Israel into the Promised Land, it was a land flowing with milk and honey. So it's interesting to note that there was a time when God changed the weather so that the region experienced desert-like conditions. After the Babylonian captivity, the Medo-Persian Empire allowed the Israelites to return to their land in peace. Upon their arrival, the people built houses for themselves. Over time, they settled back into their routines. But they neglected to rebuild the temple of God, which was the center of their spiritual life. God had brought them back into the land, but the people had forgotten about God. Haggai, a leading prophet in those days, spoke the message of God's judgment on the nation for this serious sin of neglect:

> "You looked for much, but indeed it came to little; and when you brought it home, I blew it away. Why?" says the LORD of hosts. "Because of My house that is in ruins, while every one of you runs to his own house. Therefore the heavens above you withhold the dew, and the earth withholds its fruit. For I called for a drought on the land

and the mountains, on the grain and the new wine and the oil, on whatever the ground brings forth, on men and livestock, and on all the labor of your hands" (Haggai 1:9-11).

The two messages God gives here are: 1) God judges us for our sins, including our sins of omission, or things we do not do; and 2) He is also with us even when we have sinned. The intent of His judgment is to drive us back to Him. It's interesting that a few verses later, in Haggai 2:4, God challenges the governor of Judah and the high priest by saying, "Be strong, all you people of the land…and work; for I am with you." Even in the midst of judging them He was with them.

This reminds us of Paul's words of encouragement in the New Testament: "Be strong in the Lord and in the power of his might. Put on the whole armor of God, that you may be able to stand against the wiles of the devil" (Ephesians 6:10-11). We are assured of God's help when we need it. Jesus Himself said, "I will be with you" when He gave the Great Commission:

> All authority has been given to Me in heaven and on earth. Go therefore and make disciples of all the nations, baptizing them in the name of the Father and of the Son and of the Holy Spirit, teaching them to observe all things that I have commanded you; and lo, I am with you always, even to the end of the age (Matthew 28:18-20).

That promise has never been revoked. Nor has God revoked His promise to regather the Jewish people. As Rabbi Menachem Kohen observed, from the time the Roman army destroyed Jerusalem and the temple in AD 70 to about the late nineteenth century, or some 660,000 days, the people have been scattered, and the land has experienced a similar drought-like condition with meager or no rainfall as described by Haggai. Mark Twain noted the condition of the land when he visited in 1867. But since the late 1800s, the people have started coming back, thus slowly fulfilling the parable of the fig tree. Through the twentieth century and into today, the land is well populated and is producing. The migration back into the land by the Jews from all over the world is taking place exactly as the Bible has prophesied.

Even the harshest skeptic of God's Word can see that something of great significance is taking place in our time. The Jews living in Israel today number more than 6 million people, which is a little under half of their number in the entire world (14 million). Today the land of Israel is the most arid and agriculturally productive area in the Middle East. The incredible work ethic and advanced scientific, academic, inventive, and creative abilities of the Jewish people have made them a blessing to the nations of the world, even if many don't recognize it. The Muslim nations that surround Israel are among those who fail to recognize it—they are so filled with an unnatural hatred for the Jews that they even refuse their very right to exist in the land God granted to them 4000 years ago, the land that the Bible calls "the land of Israel" (Ezekiel 11:17).

Chapter 9

The Growing Russian-Islamic Threat

As you look at the map on page 11, you can see that the tiny nation of Israel is surrounded by overwhelmingly large masses of land inhabited by hostile enemies. In addition, many Western nations and members of the United Nations pay only lip service to the idea of defending Israel from threats of violence. Over the last few decades Israel's military might and missile-defense shield have helped them to some degree, but how long will they last? In the end, only God is able to protect outnumbered Israel from its powerful enemies.

The four chapters of divinely inspired prophecy found in Ezekiel 36–39 reveal that a number of opposing nations will rise up to battle against Israel. In chapter 9 of our book *Global Warning: Are We on the Brink of World War III?* we identify Gog, Magog, and the Prince of Rosh (Ezekiel 38:2-3,15) as being the nation of present-day Russia and the army from the Middle East. The prophet Ezekiel makes it crystal clear who their intended target is in 37:10-12:

So I prophesied as He commanded me, and breath came

into them, and they lived, and stood upon their feet, an exceedingly great army. Then He said to me, "Son of man, *these bones are the whole house of Israel.* They indeed say, 'Our bones are dry, our hope is lost, and we ourselves are cut off!' Therefore prophesy and say to them, 'Thus says the Lord GOD: "Behold, O My people, I will open your graves and cause you to come up from your graves, and bring you into the land of Israel." '"

This passage describes the graveyard of bones coming to life— this is the nation of Israel. Then in verses 13-14 the prophet forecasts the time the nation will turn to God during the seven-year Tribulation and the millennium that follows:

"Then you shall know that I am the LORD, when I have opened your graves, O My people, and brought you up from your graves. I will put My Spirit in you, and you shall live, and I will place you in your own land. Then you shall know that I, the LORD, have spoken it and performed it," says the LORD.

It should not surprise us to learn that this was the position of many scholars in the early church. Most of our prophecy colleagues who take Bible prophecy literally agree with the geographical location "far north" of Israel as being the nation Russia. Then add to that the fact that Russia and the Islamic Middle Eastern nations are already functioning as allies. No other nation comes even close to Russia as a second possibility. Dr. Mark Hitchcock makes this point very clear in his article titled "Gog and Magog" in the *Tim LaHaye Prophecy Study Bible*:

The prophet Ezekiel predicted 2,600 years ago that in the latter times Israel would be furiously invaded by a people "out of the north parts" (Ezek. 38:6, 15). In Ezekiel 38:2-3; 39:1, the Hebrew word *rosh*, which simply means head, top, summit, or chief, is used to identify these people from the north. The interpretive problem is that the word *rosh* can be translated as either a proper noun or an adjective. Many translations use *rosh* as an adjective and translate it as the word "chief." I believe the better translation is to interpret *rosh* as a proper noun referring to a specific place—Russia.

The fulfillment of God's most amazing prophecies concerning Russia seems more imminent than ever before. As we track this nation in the prophecies of the End Times, we discover that her footprints lead right to the land of Israel. In tracking the events that lead to this invasion, one must consider the appearance, the allies, the activity, the annihilation, and the aftermath.

The madman called Gog by Ezekiel will be the end-time leader of Russia (38:2). A host of allies will join this leader when he invades the land of Israel (Ezek. 38:9). Eight other geographical locations are mentioned in Ezekiel 38:1-6; Meshech, Tubal, Gomer, and Togarmah (Turkey); Magog (Central Asia: Islamic southern republics of the former Soviet Union); Persia (Iran); Ethiopia or Cush (Sudan); and Libya.[1]

Why Is God "Against Russia"?

There must be special reasons that the loving and merciful God of the universe will take a stand against Russia in the latter times. History notes some of these reasons.

1. *Russia's longtime hatred for and persecution of the Jews*

Even before the Bolshevik Revolution during the Czarist monarchy, the Russian people were known for their hatred and persecution of the Jewish people. In the Pale of Settlement, Jewish people were pretty much confined by the Russian government. There, they endured so much hardship that some 30,000 Jews fled to Israel from 1881 to 1900. This is known in Jewish history as "the first Aliya," or the first ascent to Jerusalem and Palestine. At that time the land itself was in poverty and just beginning to recover from the near-drought conditions endured for some 18 centuries due to God's judgment for their rejection of the Messiah and for idolatry. During that first ascent the Zionist movement was in its earliest beginnings, and the influx of Jewish immigrants was almost more than the future state of Israel could assist. Though fleeing from Russia may have helped them to escape persecution, the Jewish people endured extreme poverty in their new homeland.

Those who stayed behind when the Russian government closed the doors to Jewish migrants lived in both poverty and loss of what freedom they had once experienced. Consequently, it's safe to conclude that due in large part to Russia's long-standing mistreatment of its Jewish population, the nation removed itself from God's eternal covenant "to bless those who bless you" (Genesis 12:3). Instead, Russia earned the other side of that prophetic promise—it earned the curse of God for their mistreatment of the Jews. Russia is still living under that curse to this day.

As we've said before, modern-day Americans should take heed of how God keeps His word regarding Genesis 12:1-3. Without a doubt the United States has experienced the blessings of God because of the help we have given to the Jews.

2. *Russia's spiteful atheism*

The spiritual revival that swept through Europe due to, among other things, the Bible being translated and printed in the languages of the common people during the Reformation had little or no impact on Russia. It has often been observed by historians that Russia missed the Renaissance, the Reformation, and most of the twentieth century! This may have been due to the repressive, dictatorial monarchies of the past and their support of the state-dominated church of Russia. Another contributing factor would be the poor education system in Russia, which means many people lacked the ability to read and share the Bible.

Unfortunately, the anti-God philosophy of socialism, the foundation of Marxism through Karl Marx, Engels, and other militant atheists, appealed to the strong nationalistic spirit of the people, leading to the Communist Revolution. This ended in the murder of the Czar and the entire Romanov family.

An interesting fact of history is that the first attempt by the Marxist socialists to overthrow the Czar back in 1905 failed despite popular opposition to the Russo-Japanese war. During World War I Kaiser Wilhelm of Germany gave permission for Lenin, a Russian exile, and his group of revolutionaries to travel across Germany in a sealed boxcar. The German leader expected these revolutionaries to sabotage the Russian army on his eastern front. Little did he dream that they would overthrow the Czarist government and then end up fighting Germany only a generation later. He was equally unaware that in aiding the revolutionaries, he was playing a role in helping to fulfill Bible prophecy. For the prophet Ezekiel, some 2500 years before, had predicted that Russia would become a major power during the end times. When the prophet made his prediction, Russia was on the fringe of civilization and populated by nomadic tribes. But from World War I onward, Russia has been a major player on the world stage.

The prophecy of Ezekiel chapters 38 and 39 affords us one of the most important predictions relating to Russia and our day. It reads almost like a daily newspaper and stands as a monument to the accuracy of the prophetic Word of God. There was a time when people laughed at those who predicted, on the basis of Ezekiel's prophecy, that Russia would someday attack Israel. Today, no one laughs at the idea, for it seems only a question of time. You may find it helpful to pause here and read Ezekiel 38–39 before proceeding. You will be amazed to see how easy it is to understand the events that are forecast. Furthermore, you will see why we can anticipate a stormy and tragic time ahead for the little nation of Israel.

3. *Russia's coalition with numerous Middle Eastern Islamic nations*

How did the obscure Hebrew prophet Ezekiel know some 2500 years ago that Israel would be back in their God-protected homeland and be opposed by hostile neighbors all around? How did he know these nations would all be driven by a very abnormal hatred and determination to exterminate Israel? We read and hear about this opposition and hatred every day in the news. Only God could have foreseen what would happen. In Isaiah 46:9-10, we read this:

> "Remember the former things of old, for I am God, and there is no other; I am God, and there is none like Me, declaring the end from the beginning, and from ancient times things that are not yet done, saying, 'My counsel shall stand, and I will do all My pleasure'" (Isaiah 46:9-10).

Truly, "there is no other." Only God could declare "the end from the beginning" and write history in advance. Only He can predict the future and have it come to pass. This proves not only that the Bible was divinely inspired, but also that He alone is the living God.

With regard to Russia's invasion of Israel, note *when* this is to take place and *where* it will take place. After listing the names of the nations that will come against Israel with warlike armaments, Ezekiel adds:

> Prepare yourself and be ready, you and all your companies that are gathered about you; and be a guard for them. After many days you will be visited. In the latter years you will come into the land of those brought back from the sword and gathered from many people on the mountains of Israel, which had long been desolate; they were brought out of the nations, and now all of them dwell safely. You will ascend, coming like a storm,

covering the land like a cloud, you and all your troops
and many peoples with you (Ezekiel 38:7-9).

Note some of the specifics here: "in the latter years," "on the mountains of Israel, which had long been desolate," and "now all of them dwell safely," which in other translations speaks of unwalled cities. How did the prophet know these conditions would exist? He didn't—not on his own! God revealed it to him through prophecy, and today we see these circumstances in place. There is far too much accurate detail for this to merely be coincidental. Again, only God can inspire His prophets to write history in advance and have it actually happen.

Not since the evil regime of Adolph Hitler—during which six million or more European Jews were mass-murdered—has there appeared a more satanically inspired group of enemies of Israel than the current Islamic terrorists. And this is exacerbated all the more by the fact Israel, a small nation, is surrounded by numerous enemy nations. Ezekiel 38 tells us there is coming a time when these enemies will attack Israel: "Thus says the Lord GOD: 'On that day it shall come to pass that thoughts will arise in your mind, and you will make an evil plan. You will say, "I will go up against a land of unwalled villages...to take plunder and to take booty...""" (38:10-12).

In March of 2011, scientists found the second largest source of oil shale in the world—in Israel. This could very well be part of the "plunder and...booty" sought by Israel's enemies in Ezekiel 38:12. This would give Russia and its Middle Eastern allies a reason to go after Israel, for the oil shale deposits would be a tremendous economic prize for the terrorists of the world. This is yet another indication that we are likely drawing near to the time of the end.

Scripture tells us that the battle between God and Satan's inspired enemies will be won not by human allies, but by God Himself. Look at Ezekiel 38:18-22:

"It will come to pass at the same time, when Gog comes against the land of Israel," says the Lord GOD, "that My fury will show in My face. For in My jealousy and in the fire of My wrath I have spoken: 'Surely in that day there shall be a great earthquake in the land of Israel, so that the fish of the sea, the birds of the heavens, the beasts of the field, all creeping things that creep on the earth, and all men who *are* on the face of the earth shall shake at My presence. The mountains shall be thrown down, the steep places shall fall, and every wall shall fall to the ground.' I will call for a sword against Gog throughout all My mountains," says the Lord GOD. "Every man's sword will be against his brother. And I will bring him to judgment with pestilence and bloodshed; I will rain down on him, on his troops, and on the many peoples who *are* with him, flooding rain, great hailstones, fire, and brimstone."

Obviously this coming battle will be won by God Himself, for only God can send a worldwide earthquake that levels mountains everywhere. This may well be the most electrifying manifestation of the existence of God Almighty since the worldwide flood in the days of Noah—a global event that changed the world forever.

There are plenty of people who doubt that the end-time prophecies in Scripture will ever take place. Their skepticism is a confirmation of biblical prophecy as well, for the apostle Peter gave this warning:

This they willfully forget: that by the word of God the heavens were of old, and the earth standing out of water and in the water, by which the world that then existed perished, being flooded with water. But the heavens and the earth which are now preserved by the same word, are reserved for fire until the day of judgment and perdition of ungodly men (2 Peter 3:5-7).

When "Gog" Meets God in Israel

The prophet Ezekiel was also led by the Spirit of God to predict the following:

> "Therefore, son of man, prophesy and say to Gog, 'Thus says the Lord GOD: "On that day when My people Israel dwell safely, will you not know it? Then you will come from your place out of the far north, you and many peoples with you, all of them riding on horses, a great company and a mighty army. You will come up against My people Israel like a cloud, to cover the land. It will be in the latter days that I will bring you against My land, so that the nations may know Me, when I am hallowed in you, O Gog, before their eyes." Thus says the Lord GOD: "Are you he of whom I have spoken in former days by My servants the prophets of Israel, who prophesied for years in those days that I would bring you against them?
>
> "And it will come to pass at the same time, when Gog comes against the land of Israel," says the Lord GOD, "that My fury will show in My face. For in My jealousy and in the fire of My wrath I have spoken: 'Surely in that day there shall be a great earthquake in the land of Israel, so that the fish of the sea, the birds of the heavens, the beasts of the field, all creeping things that creep on the earth, and all men who are on the face of the earth shall shake at My presence. The mountains shall be thrown down, the steep places shall fall, and every wall shall fall to the ground.' I will call for a sword against Gog throughout all My mountains," says the Lord God. "Every man's sword will be against his brother. And I will bring him to judgment with pestilence and bloodshed; I will rain down on him, on his troops, and on the many peoples who are with him, flooding rain, great hailstones, fire, and brimstone. Thus I will magnify Myself and sanctify Myself, and I will be known in the eyes of

many nations. Then they shall know that I am the LORD"
(38:14-23).

Almighty God, who is all-powerful in all ages and to all genera-
tions, has chosen not to demonstrate His omnipotent power during
most of world history. Instead, He has chosen, for reasons known
only to Him, to remain anonymous. Among the few exceptions
were the time when He miraculously led the close to three million
Hebrews out of slavery in Egypt and kept them alive for over 40
years while they wandered in the wilderness. Another was when He
intervened in the natural birth process of the virgin Mary to cause
His only begotten Son to be born without the impartation of the
Adamic sin nature so that He could die for the sins of the whole
world and then be raised from the dead.

When God Destroys Russia on the Mountains of Israel

Israel's very existence today, given the fact the nation is surrounded by hostile enemies, can only be attributed to the protective
hand of God in fulfillment of His promise in Genesis 12:1-3. Israel
has been supernaturally preserved multiple times when attacked by
large, well-equipped armies. Yet after more than 60 years, they still
occupy their land in troubled times, just as the prophets predicted.

Many people argue that Russia continues to show signs of both
resistance and strength in its efforts to reestablish the Soviet Union.
And given Russia's relationships with the hostile Arab neighbors
surrounding Israel—which includes Iran, with its ongoing nuclear
development—we are seeing things come together in a way that
appears to indicate we're coming closer to the fulfillment of Bible
prophecy.

However, we have no reason to fear! For Bible prophecy also
foretells God will not allow Israel to be destroyed again. He has
promised to save Israel and destroy the invading enemies "on the

mountains of Israel" (Ezekiel 37:8). Why? So all the world will know He is God!

This future divine intervention by God is for more than just saving Israel, though this is very important. It is also to, once and for all, just before the end times begin, demonstrate to a skeptical world that there is indeed a God in heaven who is all-powerful and in control of all that happens on earth.

Why will this take place? There are eight statements in Ezekiel chapters 38 and 39 that explain the reason for God's planned destruction of Russia and its allies. Consider the following carefully:

38:16—You will come up against My people Israel like a cloud, to cover the land. It will be in the latter days that I will bring you against My land, *so that the nations may know Me*, when I am hallowed in you, O Gog, before their eyes.

38:23—I will magnify Myself and sanctify Myself, and I will be known in the eyes of many nations. *Then they shall know that I am the LORD.*

39:6—I will send fire on Magog and on those who live in security in the coastlands. *Then they shall know that I am the LORD.*

39:7—I will make My holy name known in the midst of My people Israel, and I will not let them profane My holy name anymore. *Then the nations shall know that I am the LORD, the Holy One in Israel.*

39:22—The house of Israel *shall know that I am the LORD their God* from that day forward.

39:27—When I have brought them back from the peoples and gathered them out of their enemies' lands, and *I am hallowed* in them in the sight of many nations...

39:28—...then *they shall know that I am the LORD their God*, who sent them into captivity among the nations, but also brought them back to their land, and left none of them captive any longer.

There is no question that when Russia and her allies come down against little Israel to wipe her out, God will both rescue her supernaturally and also prove that He alone is the Lord God of the universe. In fact, in the scriptures above He singles out four groups—mainly atheists and those who forget or reject God. He is the Creator of all things as well as the Sustainer of our present world. He repeatedly cites "the nations may know" or "they shall know." In Ezekiel 39:6-7 God said,

> I will send fire on Magog and on those who live in security in the coastlands. Then they shall know that I am the LORD. So I will make My holy name known in the midst of My people Israel, and I will not let them profane My holy name anymore. Then the nations shall know that I am the LORD, the Holy One in Israel.

"In security in the coastlands" suggests God will defeat even the secret terrorists who come against Israel. He will protect Israel from even clandestine efforts against it. God's intervention will save Israel and rescue it from every possible attempt made against it.

In light of the fact God will make Himself obvious and that the nations will know it is He who is protecting Israel, no one will be without excuse when it comes time to give an account to God. Those who are not believers and who reject Jesus as the Savior will have seen God's supernatural hand of intervention at work. They will know that the preservation of Israel is an act of God.

Tragically, as Bible prophecy clearly indicates, there will be many people who willfully reject Him and do not surrender their lives to Him. That will be a dreadful mistake for those individuals, for their decision will prohibit them from experiencing the wonderful blessings God has in store during both the 1000-year kingdom of peace and eternity.

Will the Rapture Occur Before or After Russia's Destruction?

One common question asked by people who want to understand Bible prophecy is, "When will the destruction of Russia occur—before the rapture, or after?" We do not think the Bible makes this crystal clear. However, it is worth noting that Scripture never tells Christians to watch for the coming of the Tribulation or the Antichrist (who, by the way, could be in the world today—after all, there are many ways in which our world is moving toward the one-world government that he will one day rule over). The fact we are not to anticipate the Tribulation is one of many reasons it makes sense for the rapture to occur before the Tribulation.

Russia's destruction is a Tribulation event, so it won't occur until after the "blessed hope," or the rapture. But it will take place before His "glorious appearing" (Titus 2:12-13), which, according to Jesus, will come "immediately after the tribulation of those days" (Matthew 24:29). We do not know when Christ will come to rapture His church, but there can be no doubt that the second phase of His second coming, which is "the glorious appearing," will be "immediately after the tribulation of those days." That is why we as Christians can say, "We are not looking for the Antichrist; we are looking for the Lord Jesus Christ!"

According to Daniel 9:27, the Antichrist will attain his power through diplomacy (which is why he has a bow without arrows in Revelation 6:2). He will make a covenant for seven years with the nation of Israel—this will occur at the beginning of the Tribulation. Therefore, Israel will be alive and well at this time. Those Jewish people who are Christians will be raptured along with all believing Gentiles (non-Jews). First Thessalonians 5:9-11 affirms that all believers will be taken up in the rapture because "God did not appoint us to wrath":

> God did not appoint us to wrath, but to obtain salvation through our Lord Jesus Christ, who died for us,

that whether we wake or sleep, we should live together with Him. Therefore comfort each other and edify one another, just as you also are doing (1 Thessalonians 5:9-11).

Secular Jews, however, will be left behind after the rapture of the church, and they will be among those who are in support of the seven-year covenant of peace under the leadership of the Antichrist.

So the events of Ezekiel 38 will likely take place after the rapture, although nothing in Scripture prohibits them from occurring before the rapture. That's why we say the Bible isn't crystal clear on this. But ultimately, God's miraculous rescue of the Jewish nation will result in many Jews coming to faith in Jesus as the true Messiah.

CHAPTER 10

The Triumphant
Return of Israel's Messiah

We've spoken about the rapture and the many judgments that will take place during the seven years of the Tribulation. But when will Christ make His return to earth? At what point will His glorious appearing take place?

For Christians, the second coming of Christ is the most highly anticipated event in the history of the world. The "glorious appearing" (Titus 2:13) is the ultimate fulfillment of Christ's promised return. When He returns, there will be no need to debate His claims or His message. The arrival of the King will end all speculation and usher in a time of unprecedented worship by His followers.

The account of this glorious appearing, which appears in Revelation 19, is among the most dramatic chapters in the Bible. It stands as an exclamation mark at the end of the redeeming work of Christ. In Revelation 19, Jesus Christ returns to earth to crush His enemies and establish His kingdom. It is at this time that the fulfillment of the many yet future prophecies regarding His reign will finally come to pass.

The Events of the Glorious Appearing

To be clear, the glorious appearing is not just a single event but rather a series of events that will take place at the end of the seven-year Tribulation. The following activities appear to best represent the predictions made throughout Scripture for this time:

1. It takes place immediately after the Tribulation (Matthew 24:29).

2. Cosmic phenomena will occur in the sun, moon, and stars (Matthew 24:29).

3. The sign of the Son of Man in heaven will be seen by everyone (Matthew 24:30), and Christ will gather His elect (verse 31).

4. Heaven will open and Christ will appear on a white horse (Revelation 19:11).

5. Christ will be followed by the armies of heaven (Revelation 19:14), prepared to judge the ungodly (Jude 4-15).

6. Christ will come in power and great glory (Matthew 24:30).

7. Christ will stand on the Mount of Olives (Zechariah 14:3-5).

8. Unbelievers will mourn, for they are not ready (Matthew 24:30).

9. The beast (Antichrist) and his armies will confront Christ (Revelation 19:19).

10. Christ will cast the beast and false prophet into the lake of fire (Revelation 19:20).

11. Christ's rejecters will be killed (Revelation 19:21).

12. Satan will be cast into the bottomless pit for 1000 years (Revelation 20:1-3).

13. The Old Testament and Tribulation saints will be resurrected (Matthew 24:31; Revelation 20:4).

14. Christ will judge the nations and establish His kingdom (Matthew 25).

Are the Rapture and the Glorious Appearing the Same Event or Two Different Events?

The return of Christ will have two phases—the rapture, in which the church is taken up to heaven before the Tribulation, and the return, in which Christ and the church will descend victoriously upon the earth. That there are two phases is very evident when we observe that there are at least 15 differences in the descriptions of Christ's coming that cannot be reconciled into one event.

The 15 Differences Between the Rapture and the Glorious Appearing

Rapture/Blessed Hope	Glorious Appearing
1. Christ comes in the air for His own	1. Christ comes with His own to earth
2. Rapture of all Christians	2. No one raptured
3. Christians taken to the Father's house	3. Resurrected saints do not see Father's house
4. No judgment on earth	4. Christ judges inhabitants of earth
5. Church taken to heaven	5. Christ sets up His kingdom on earth

Rapture/Blessed Hope	Glorious Appearing
6. Imminent—could happen at any moment	6. Cannot occur for at least 7 years
7. No signs	7. Many signs for Christ's physical coming
8. For believers only	8. Affects all humanity
9. Time of joy	9. Time of mourning
10. Before the "day of wrath" (Tribulation)	10. Immediately after Tribulation (Matthew 24)
11. No mention of Satan	11. Satan bound in abyss for 1000 years
12. The judgment seat of Christ	12. No time or place for judgment seat
13. Marriage of the Lamb	13. His bride descends with Him
14. Only His own see Him	14. Every eye will see Him
15. Tribulation begins	15. 1000-year kingdom of Christ begins

Source: *Essential Guide to Bible Prophecy* (Eugene, OR: Harvest House, 2006/2012), pp. 53-54.

The rapture will take place at any moment because it is the next event on God's prophetic calendar. The glorious appearing of Jesus Christ will occur at the end of the Tribulation. Christ addressed this time in Matthew 24, a passage we have looked at earlier in this book. Just before the crucifixion, the disciples asked Jesus, "What will be the sign of Your coming, and of the end of the age?" (Matthew 24:3). In His reply our Lord said, "Immediately after the tribulation of those days…the powers of the heavens will be shaken. Then the sign of the Son of Man will appear in heaven, and then all the tribes of the earth will mourn, and they will see the Son of Man coming on the clouds of heaven with power and great glory" (Matthew 24:29-30).

As Jesus looked down the corridor of time to the end of the present age, He warned of a time of great tribulation that would come upon the whole world (Matthew 24:5-28). Our Lord went on to explain that the devastation that takes place will be so extensive that unless those days were cut short, "no flesh would be saved" (Matthew 24:22). Jesus further described this coming day of trouble as a time when the sun and moon will be darkened and "the powers of the heavens will be shaken" (Matthew 24:29). His description runs parallel to that found in Revelation 16:1-16, where the final hour of the Tribulation is depicted by atmospheric darkness, air pollution, and ecological disaster.

The return of Christ will mark both the total defeat of the Antichrist and the total triumph of Christ. Without Christ, there is no hope of a better future. He is the central figure of the world to come. It is His kingdom, and all believers in Him are prophetically referred to as "the bride of Christ."

The Promise of Christ's Return

Jesus promised His disciples, in the upper room, that He was going to heaven to prepare a place for them. Then He said, "If I go and prepare a place for you, I will come again, and receive you unto myself; that where I am, there ye may be also" (John 14:3 KJV). Even though the early disciples eventually died, the Bible promised, "Behold, I shew you a mystery; we shall not all sleep [die], but we shall all be changed [resurrected or raptured], in a moment, in the twinkling of an eye, at the last trump: for the trumpet shall sound, and the dead shall be raised incorruptible, and we shall be changed" (1 Corinthians 15:51-52 KJV).

The apostle Paul reiterated this same hope in 1 Thessalonians 4:13-17, where he commented about those believers who have already died and gone to heaven. He said,

> If we believe that Jesus died and rose again, even so God will bring with Him those who sleep [die] in Jesus...For the Lord Himself will descend from heaven with a shout, with the voice of an archangel, and with the trump of God. And the dead in Christ will rise first. Then we who are alive and remain shall be caught up together with them in the clouds to meet the Lord in the air (verses 14-17).

The promise to return for the church (believers of the church age) is a promise of the rapture. Jesus' specific promise to return personally and physically to take His church up to heaven guarantees that fact! When Revelation 19 opens, the church is already in heaven with Christ at the marriage supper. The rapture has already occurred. Jesus is depicted as the groom and the church as the bride. The marriage supper celebrates their union after the rapture and before their return to earth.

One of the greatest interpretive problems for those who do not believe in the rapture of the church is to explain how the church got to heaven prior to the second coming. Surely they are not all martyred off, or else Paul's comment about "we who are alive and remain" (1 Thessalonians 4:15) would be meaningless. The rapture must be presumed to have occurred before the events in Revelation 19—amillennialists and postmillennialists notwithstanding!

The position of the church (bride of the Lamb) in Revelation 19:7-10 in heaven is crucial to the interpretation of the entire apocalypse. The church is not mentioned during the seal, trumpet, and bowl judgments because the church is not on earth during the outpouring of these judgments. The term "church" (Greek, *ekklesia*) appears frequently in Revelation chapters 1–3. In fact, it is used

19 times in those chapters. But the word "church" does not appear again until Revelation 22:16—and the reason is because it's not on the earth. In the meantime, the church appears in Revelation 19:7-10 as the bride of the Lamb.

The concept of the church as the bride or wife of Christ is clearly stated in Ephesians 5:25-26, where husbands are admonished to love their wives as Christ loved the church and gave Himself for her that He might present her in heaven as a glorious bride. There can be no doubt, therefore, that John—in Revelation—intends for us to see the Lamb's "wife" as the church—the bride of Christ. This of course will include all who have accepted the crucified Christ—Jews and Gentiles.

The Nature of Christ's Return

Jesus not only promised to return for His church; He also promised to return to judge the world and to establish His kingdom on earth. His half brother James referred to believers as "heirs of the kingdom which He promised to those who love him" (James 2:5). Jesus Himself told His disciples that He would not drink the fruit of the vine after the last supper until He drank it with them in His Father's kingdom (Matthew 26:29). After the resurrection, the disciples asked Jesus, "Lord, will You at this time restore the kingdom to Israel?" (Acts 1:6). Jesus replied that the time was in the Father's hand. All these references imply a future kingdom when Christ returns.

The details of Christ's return are as follows:

He will return personally. The Bible says that "the Lord Himself will descend from heaven" (1 Thessalonians 4:16). Jesus promised He will return in person (Matthew 24:30).

He will appear as the Son of Man. Since Pentecost, Christ has ministered through the Holy Spirit (John 14:16-23; 16:7-20). But when He returns to earth, He will appear as the Son of Man in His glorified human form (Matthew 24:30; 26:64; see also Daniel 7:13-14).

He will return literally and visibly. In Acts 1:11, the angels promised, "This same Jesus, who was taken up from you into heaven, will
so come in like manner." Revelation 1:7 tells us, "Every eye will see
him, even they who pierced Him. And all the tribes of the earth will
mourn." Nowhere in Scripture is there a suggestion that Christ's
second coming in power and great glory will be anything but visible and physical. In fact, all unbelievers on the earth at the time of
Christ's return will be eyewitnesses to it. Preterists, who claim Christ
has already returned, cannot point to any past time when anyone
has ever witnessed such.

He will come suddenly and dramatically. Paul warned, "The day of
the Lord so comes as a thief in the night" (1 Thessalonians 5:2). Jesus
said, "As the lightning comes from the east and flashes to the west,
so also will the coming of the Son of Man be" (Matthew 24:27).

He will come on the clouds of heaven. Jesus said, "They will see
the Son of Man coming on the clouds of heaven" (Matthew 24:30).
Daniel 7:13 makes the same prediction. So does Luke 21:27. Revelation 1:7 says, "Behold, He is coming with clouds."

He will come in a display of glory. Matthew 16:27 promises, "The
Son of Man will come in the glory of His Father." Matthew 24:30
adds, "They will see the Son of Man coming…with power and
great glory."

He will come with all His angels. Jesus promised He would "send
His angels with a great sound of a trumpet" (Matthew 24:31). He
said in one of His parables, "The reapers are the angels…so it will
be at the end of this age" (Matthew 13:39-40).

He will come with His bride, the church. That, of course, is
the whole point of Revelation 19. Colossians 3:4 adds, "When
Christ…appears, then you also will appear with Him in glory."
Zechariah 14:5 says, "The LORD my God will come, and all the
saints with You."

He will return to the Mount of Olives. "In that day His feet will
stand on the Mount of Olives" (Zechariah 14:4). Where the glory

of God ascended into heaven, it will return (Ezekiel 11:23). Where Jesus ascended into heaven, He will return (Acts 1:9-11).

He will return in triumph and victory. Zechariah 14:9 states, "The LORD shall be King over all the earth." Revelation 19:16 depicts Him as "King of kings and Lord of lords." He will triumph over the Antichrist, the false prophet, and Satan (Revelation 19:19-21).

Revelation 19 opens with a heavenly chorus of "a great multitude" singing the praises of God (verse 1). The heavenly choir rejoices with praise because justice has finally been served. "True and righteous are His judgments," they sing, "because He has judged the great harlot" (verse 2). The praise chorus then breaks into a fourfold alleluia in verses 1-6:

> "Alleluia! Salvation and glory and power belong to the Lord our God" (verse 1).

> "Alleluia! Her smoke rises up forever and ever!" (verse 3).

> They "worshiped God…on the throne, saying, 'Amen! Alleluia!'" (verse 4).

> "Alleluia! For the Lord God Omnipotent reigns!" (verse 6).

The Marriage upon Christ's Return

The marriage of the Lamb is announced suddenly and dramatically. It is as though we have finally arrived at what we have been waiting for all along. The wedding is finally here. It is obvious that John the revelator views this as a future (not past) event. The church is the betrothed bride of Christ now, but our marriage to Him is in the future.

This is why we cannot say that the consummation of the marriage has already taken place. The apostle Paul wrote, "I have betrothed you to one husband, that I may present you as a chaste virgin to Christ" (2 Corinthians 11:2). He also said that Christ "loved the church and gave Himself for her…that He might present her to Himself a glorious church, not having spot or wrinkle or any such thing, but that she should be holy and without blemish" (Ephesians 5:25-27).

The New Testament pictures the church as engaged to Christ at this present time. We are still awaiting the "judgment seat of Christ" (2 Corinthians 5:10), presumably after the rapture and before the marriage supper. The marriage ceremony itself will follow in heaven while the Tribulation is taking place here on earth.

While Revelation 19 pictures Christ symbolically as the Lamb (verse 7), the picture of the marriage is clearly expressed. The aorist tense of "has come" (Greek, *elthen*) indicates a completed act, showing that the wedding is now consummated. Instead of the normal seven-day Jewish wedding ceremony, this one presumably lasts seven years (during the Tribulation period). The marriage is completed in heaven (Revelation 19:7), but the marriage supper will probably take place later on earth, where Israel is awaiting the return of Christ and the church.

This is the only way to distinguish the Bridegroom (Christ), the bride (church), and the ten virgins (Israel) in Matthew 25:1-13. There is no way that He is coming to marry all ten (or five) of these women. They are the attendants (Old Testament saints and Tribulation saints) at the wedding. Only the church is the bride. That is why Jesus could say of John the Baptist that there was not a "greater prophet" (Old Testament saint), but that the "least in the kingdom of God" (New Testament church) is "greater than he" (Luke 7:28).

The Triumph of Christ's Return

The picture of Christ's return in Revelation 19:11-16 is one of the most dramatic passages in the entire Bible! In these six verses we are swept up into the triumphal entourage of redeemed saints as they ride in the heavenly procession with the King of kings and Lord of lords. In this one passage alone, all the hopes and dreams of every believer are finally and fully realized. This is not the Palm Sunday procession with the humble Messiah on the donkey colt. This is the ultimate in eschatological drama. The rejected Savior returns in triumph as the rightful King of all the world—and we are with Him.

The description of the triumphant Savior is that of a king leading an army to victory. The context of the passage itself includes the final phase of the seventh bowl of judgment begun in Revelation 16:17-21, and moves through the details of 17:1–18:24 and on to chapter 19.

As the scene unfolds, heaven opens to reveal Christ followed by the army of the redeemed. The description of their being clad in white (Revelation 19:14) emphasizes the garments of the bride already mentioned earlier (verse 8). In this vignette, the bride appears as the army of the Messiah. But unlike contemporary apocalyptic dramas of that time (for example, the War Scroll of the Qumran sect), the victory is won without any military help from the faithful. This army has no weapons, no swords, no shields, no armor. They are merely clad in the "righteous acts of the saints" (verse 8). They have not come to fight, but to watch. They have not come to assist, but to celebrate. The Messiah-King will do the fighting. He alone will win the battle by the power of His spoken word.

The twelvefold description of the coming King combines elements of symbolism from various Bible passages and from the other pictures of the risen Christ in the book of Revelation. Notice the details of His appearance:

1. He is called faithful and true (Revelation 3:14).

2. He judges and makes war in righteousness (2 Thessalonians 1:7-8).

3. His eyes are as a flame of fire (Revelation 1:14).

4. He wears many crowns (Revelation 4:10).

5. His name is unknown—a wonderful secret (Judges 13:18; Isaiah 9:6).

6. He is clothed in a robe dipped in blood (Isaiah 63:1-6).

7. His name is called the Word of God (John 1:1).

8. A sharp sword is in His mouth (Revelation 19:15).

9. He rules with a rod of iron (Psalm 2:9).

10. He treads the winepress of the wrath of God (Isaiah 63:1-6; Revelation 14:14-20).

11. His written name is King of kings and Lord of lords (Daniel 2:47; Revelation 17:14).

There can be no doubt that the rider on the white horse in Revelation 19:11-16 is Jesus Christ. He comes as the apostle Paul predicted: "in flaming fire taking vengeance on those who do not know God…[who] shall be punished with everlasting destruction…when He comes, in that Day, to be glorified in His saints and to be admired among all those who believe" (2 Thessalonians 1:8-10).

This is the true Christ (Messiah) not the usurper (Antichrist). He rides the white horse of conquest, and His victory is sure. His greatness is in the spiritual qualities of His person: He is faithful, true, righteous. His eyes of fire penetrate our sinfulness and expose our spiritual inadequacy. His "many crowns" were probably received from the redeemed, who will cast them at His feet in worship (Revelation 4:10). The fact that these crowns are many totally upstages the seven crowns of the dragon (Revelation 12:3) and the ten crowns of the beast (Revelation 13:1). His unknown name is a secret or "wonder" (see Judges 13:18; Isaiah 9:6). He is Jehovah God Himself—the Yahweh of the Old Testament. He is the I Am whose name is "above every name" (Philippians 2:9).

John wants us to know for certain who this is, so he calls Jesus by his favorite name: the Word (Greek, *logos*) of God (see John 1:1). Christ is the self-disclosure of the Almighty. He is the personal revelation of God to man. He is the personal Word who is also the author of the written Word. The One revealed is the ultimate revelator of the revelation: Jesus the Christ.

When the Savior returns, He will come from heaven with His bride at His side. The church militant will be the church triumphant. Her days of conflict, rejection, and persecution will be over. She will return victorious with her Warrior-King-Husband.

Every true believer who reads the prediction of Christ's triumphal return in Revelation 19:11-16 should be overwhelmed by its significance. Think about it: We will be in that heavenly army with Him when He returns from glory. In fact, if you are a Christian, you might want to take a pen and circle the word "armies" in Revelation 19:14 and write your name in the margin next to the verse, for you will be there when He returns!

The destiny of the believer is now fully clarified. Our future hope includes 1) the rapture, 2) Christ's return, and 3) Christ's reign. The church must be raptured to heaven prior to the marriage and prior to her return from heaven with Christ. In the rapture, we will go up to heaven. In the return, we will come back to earth. And in the millennium, we will reign with Christ on the earth for 1000 years (Revelation 20:4).

The Authority of the King of Kings

In Revelation 19:15, we read, "Now out of His mouth goes a sharp sword, that with it He should strike the nations. And He Himself will rule them with a rod of iron." Christ will come victorious, and strike down His enemies. His glorious appearing with the heavenly armies will not only bring to consummation the enmity of Satan, his Antichrist, the false prophet, and the millions they deceive, but it will also usher in the righteous reign of Christ on earth. This fact is seen clearly in the name given to Christ in verse 16: "King of kings and Lord of lords."

A warrior goes into battle with his sword on his thigh; Christ's sword will be His spoken word. The word that called the world into being will call human leaders and the armies of all nations into control. And Christ Jesus, the living Lord, will be established in that day for what He is in reality: King above all kings, Lord above all lords. The prophet Zechariah said it best: "The Lord shall be King over all the earth. In that day it shall be—'The Lord is one,' and His name one" (Zechariah 14:9). Amen!

Chapter 11

The Future Millennial Kingdom

The glorious appearing of Jesus Christ as Israel's Messiah will begin the time described in Bible prophecy as the millennium. This 1000-year period is described in Revelation 20:1-6 as follows:

> Then I saw an angel coming down from heaven, having the key to the bottomless pit and a great chain in his hand. He laid hold of the dragon, that serpent of old, who is the Devil and Satan, and bound him for a *thousand years*; and he cast him into the bottomless pit, and shut him up, and set a seal on him, so that he should deceive the nations no more till the *thousand years* were finished. But after these things he must be released for a little while.

> And I saw thrones, and they sat on them, and judgment was committed to them. Then I saw the souls of those who had been beheaded for their witness to Jesus and for the word of God, who had not worshiped the beast or his image, and had not received his mark on their

foreheads or on their hands. And they lived and reigned
with Christ for a *thousand years*. But the rest of the dead
did not live again until the *thousand years* were finished.
This is the first resurrection. Blessed and holy is he who
has part in the first resurrection. Over such the second
death has no power, but they shall be priests of God and
of Christ, and shall reign with Him a *thousand years*.

Just how long will this kingdom last? There is only one chapter
in the Bible that reveals this information, and that is Revelation 20.
There, we find the phrase "thousand years" mentioned six times in
the first seven verses. More specifically, verse 6 says, "Blessed and
holy is he who has part in the first resurrection. Over such the second death has no power, but they shall be priests of God and of
Christ, and shall reign with Him a thousand years."

Throughout the Old and New Testaments are numerous references to the kingdom of Christ, the long-anticipated time when
the Lord Jesus Himself will reign upon the earth. This is, in fact,
one of the more frequently mentioned subjects in the Bible. Many
names are used to describe this period, including the kingdom age,
the age of peace, the reign of Christ, and the millennium. Not to
be confused with the eternal realm of heaven, this temporary kingdom will be a time of peace on earth, which mankind has always
yearned for.

Throughout the centuries, every scheme devised by man to forge
a utopian world has failed. Why? There are two reasons: First, man
has a sinful and degenerate heart and cannot produce a world of
peace, no matter how hard he tries. Second, as long as Satan is roam-
ing free on the earth, there will always be war. He is not only a
deceiver, but a hater of people who continues to pit nations against
each other. The proliferation of war even in this era of the United
Nations is evidence that man will always fail in his attempts to secure
peace. The United Nations was established to help bring about a
permanent discontinuation of war. However, since its inception,

there have been more wars and more bloodshed than in any comparable period of world history.

When Jesus taught His followers in Matthew 6:10 to pray "Thy kingdom come" (KJV), He was referring specifically to the millennial kingdom. It will certainly be the most incredible kingdom in all of human history—a kingdom in which Jesus, the anointed King, will have the nations for His inheritance (Psalm 2:8), when "the wolf also shall dwell with the lamb" (Isaiah 11:6), and "the earth shall be full of the knowledge of the LORD" (Isaiah 11:9).

Understanding the Millennium

The word *millennium* is a Latin term that means "a thousand years." Despite the many biblical references to the millennial reign of Christ, and despite the fact that Christians will play a vital role in it, most believers know very little about this critical period in our planet's future. Before we find out more about this kingdom, let's first examine the three major views people have held historically regarding the millennial kingdom.

Premillennialism is the belief that the second coming of Christ to set up His earthly kingdom will occur prior to the millennial age. This is the view accepted by nearly all Bible scholars who take the Scriptures literally and at face value whenever possible.

Dr. Clarence Larkin, in his masterful book *Dispensational Truth*, offers the following evidence:

1. When Christ comes He will raise the dead, but the Righteous dead are to be raised before the Millennium, that they may reign with Christ during the 1,000 years, hence there can be no Millennium before Christ comes (Revelation 20:5).

2. When Christ comes He will separate the "tares" from the "wheat," but as the Millennium is a period of universal righteousness the separation of the "tares" and "wheat"

must take place before the Millennium, therefore there can be no Millennium before Christ's physical return to the Earth (Matthew 13:40-43).

3. When Christ comes Satan shall be bound, but as Satan is to be bound during the Millennium, there can be no Millennium until Christ comes (Revelation 20:1-3).

4. When Christ comes Antichrist is to be destroyed, but as Antichrist is to come before the Millennium there can be no Millennium until Christ comes (2 Thessalonians 2:8; Revelation 19:20).

5. When Christ comes the Jews are to be restored to their own land, but as they are to be restored to their own land before the Millennium, there can be no Millennium before Christ comes (Ezekiel 36:24-28; Revelation 1:7; Zechariah 12:10).

6. When Christ comes it will be unexpectedly, and we are commanded to watch lest He take us unawares. Now if He is not coming until after the Millennium, and the Millennium is not yet here, why command us to watch for an event that is over 1,000 years off?[1]

There are others who believe the world is going to become more and more "Christianized" in time and, as a result, will usher in the kingdom of Christ on its own merits. In this scenario, Jesus would return at the end of the millennium to an already-righteous earth. This belief is known as *postmillennialism*.

A third viewpoint, known as *amillennialism*, holds to a nonliteral or spiritualized interpretation of Scripture and attempts to allegorically explain away the coming millennium. In the amillennial scheme, there is no anticipation of a literal reign of Christ on earth.

The early Christians were unquestionably premillennialists. In fact, the disciples and those whom they taught anticipated the

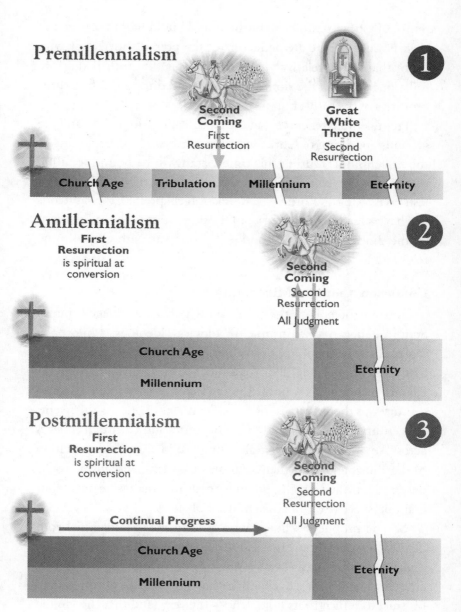

Premillennialism

Second Coming
First Resurrection

Great White Throne
Second Resurrection

Church Age | Tribulation | Millennium | Eternity

Amillennialism

First Resurrection
is spiritual at conversion

Second Coming
Second Resurrection
All Judgment

Church Age
Millennium
Eternity

Postmillennialism

First Resurrection
is spiritual at conversion

Continual Progress

Second Coming
Second Resurrection
All Judgment

Church Age
Millennium
Eternity

Excerpted and adapted from Tim LaHaye and Thomas Ice, *Charting the End Times* (Eugene, OR: Harvest House Publishers, 2001), p. 129.

return of Christ and the establishment of His kingdom on earth in their lifetime. There are detractors of the premillennial view who claim that it is a relatively new theory, but the truth is that pre-millennialism was the dominant view held during the first three centuries of the early church.

Premillennilists believe that the rapture, the Tribulation, and the glorious appearing of Christ will all occur before the beginning of the millennium. During this time, Satan will be bound for 1000 years and a theocratic kingdom of peace on earth will ensue, with Jesus as its King. According to Revelation chapter 20, the righteous will have already been raised from the dead prior to the millennium (at the time of the rapture) and will participate with Christ in the reign of His kingdom.

Confusion About the Millennium

Toward the end of the third century AD, the allegorizing of Scripture began to consume theological ideology. Philosophy replaced the study of Scripture, and premillennialism, along with many other important biblical teachings (such as salvation by grace), fell into disrepute. Not until after the Reformation of the sixteenth century was there a revival of premillennial thought. As the twenti-eth century began to unfold, Bible institutes and Christian colleges across America sprang up emphasizing a solid, literal interpretation of the Bible, and with them, a return to premillennialism. Today, despite continued attacks, premillennialism remains the most dom-inant perspective of the three millennial views.

Several prophecy scholars who hold to the premillennial com-ing of Christ position (such as Dr. Thomas Ice) also point out that premillennialists have been a great force within the evangelical church when it comes to championing the biblically affirmed right of Israel to return to its homeland—the very land that the United Nations officially recognized as the sovereign State of Israel in 1948. So it's difficult to understand how, at this late date in the unfolding of God's plan for His chosen people, some younger evangelicals have succumbed to the heresy that this land is the home of the Palestinians, who are not an ethnic people, but are Arabs. Most of these Arabs are fiercely anti-Semitic and are committed to the utter destruction of Israel. Before they can carry out their desire, however, they must win the approval of the United States and especially the Christian evangelicals in it. We pray that will never happen!

Amillennialism holds that there will be no literal kingdom on the earth following the second coming of Christ. It tends to spiritualize and allegorize all prophecies concerning the millennium, and yet-to-be-fulfilled prophecies relating to Israel are attributed to the church instead. Amillennialists also believe Satan was bound during Christ's first appearance on earth 2000 years ago, an argument that can hardly be substantiated when one considers the present condition of our world and Peter's observation that "the devil walks about like a roaring lion" (1 Peter 5:8).

Furthermore, amillennialists aren't sure whether the millennium is being fulfilled currently on earth or whether it's being fulfilled by the saints in heaven. However, they tend to agree that our current state of affairs is probably as good as the world is going to get and that the eternal realm, not the millennial kingdom, will immediately follow the second coming of Christ. Those who hold to this view go to great lengths to avoid the simple and plain literal interpretation of Scripture regarding the binding of Satan and the reign of Christ for 1000 years on earth (Revelation 20:2-7).

Postmillennialism is the belief that the world will continue to get better and better until the entire globe is Christianized, at which time Christ will return to a kingdom already flourishing in peace. Although this view was popular at the beginning of the twentieth century, it has all but died out as a result of the World Wars, the Great Depression, and the overwhelming escalation of moral evil in our society. However, those of the preterist persuasion are making a concerted attempt to resuscitate the postmillennial theory, but are not gaining much headway primarily because most lay people who read the Bible tend to take it literally. And if one takes Bible prophecy literally, it becomes apparent that the world will continue to get worse, not better, prior to the millennium.

The Premillennial Hope

According to the premillennial view, the rapture of the church, followed by the Tribulation and the glorious appearing of Jesus, will take place prior to Christ's establishment of His 1000-year kingdom. As the prophet Isaiah predicted:

> Unto us a Child is born, unto us a Son is given; and the government will be upon His shoulder. And His name will be called Wonderful, Counselor, Mighty God, Everlasting Father, Prince of Peace. Of the increase of His government and peace there will be no end (Isaiah 9:6).

While the first part of this prophecy was fulfilled during Christ's first appearance on earth, the second part has yet to be fulfilled. At no time was the government on Jesus' shoulder when He was here 2000 years ago, nor has there ever been a global government of peace. This kingdom will occur when our Lord returns to the earth at His second coming and establishes His millennial reign on earth (Revelation 5:10).

Many of the one-world government advocates today believe that the only hope for world peace in our time is to have a world dictator. From a biblical standpoint, no mere human being is competent to fill such a position. History has proven time and again that power corrupts and absolute power corrupts absolutely. If a man were to be given the role of world dictator (which will, in fact, occur for a short time during the horrifying Tribulation period that immediately precedes the millennium), inevitably everything would fall apart. The earth requires a holy, loving, merciful leader who will treat all people equitably. Jesus Christ alone qualifies for that role, and until He comes, the world will never know true peace.

How Will the Millennial Kingdom Begin?

After the last of the judgments at the conclusion of the seven-year Tribulation, the Lord will appear in the sky for all to see. He will be accompanied by the angels and by His bride, the church: "Behold, He is coming with clouds, and every eye will see Him, even they who pierced Him. And all the tribes of the earth will mourn because of Him" (Revelation 1:7).

The glorious appearing of Jesus Christ in the clouds will signal the beginning of the millennial era. At this point, the Battle of Armageddon will end, the Antichrist will be cast into the lake of fire, and Satan will be bound for the duration of the 1000-year kingdom. Jesus will also divide the remaining survivors of the Tribulation into two groups:

> When the Son of Man comes in His glory, and all the holy angels with Him, then He will sit on the throne of His glory. All the *nations* will be gathered before Him, and He will separate them one from another, as a shepherd divides his sheep from the goats. And He will set the sheep on His right hand, but the goats on the left. Then the King will say to those on His right hand, "Come, you blessed of My Father, *inherit the kingdom* prepared for you from the foundation of the world" (Matthew 25:31-34).

The "goats" mentioned here are the millions of unsaved and unbelieving followers of the Antichrist who took the mark of the beast, persecuted the Jews, and killed the Christians during the Tribulation. They will immediately be cast into hell. The "sheep" are those Gentile individuals who refused to take the mark and befriended and protected the Jews during this period. It is these surviving Jews and Gentiles who will enter the millennial kingdom in their natural bodies and repopulate the earth during the 1000 years of Christ's rule.

The other group of people who will occupy the earth during the millennium will be those with immortal, resurrected bodies. This would include everyone who received a new body at the time of the rapture and the Tribulation saints who are to be resurrected at the appearance of Christ. It is quite probable that it will also include Gentile believers whom Jesus said would "sit down with Abraham, Isaac, and Jacob in the kingdom" (Matthew 8:11). This group will not procreate, but will rule and reign with Christ during this period of time. Only those who exist in their natural bodies will have the ability to procreate.

During the millennium, Jesus, the Holy Judge, will reign supreme. His kingdom will be one of righteousness. Since Satan is bound for the duration, there will be no deception (although at the end of the millennium, Satan will be released for a brief time before being bound for eternity). This era will be a time of global peace without any fear of fellow man. It will also be a time of longevity. People's lifespans will increase dramatically; consequently, the earth's population could reach unprecedented numbers, most of whom will be believers in Christ.

One of the characteristics of our present time is that so few people really know about God and the Bible. But during the millennium, it won't be necessary to preach the gospel anymore because those who dwell on the earth will instinctively know it:

> I will put My law in their minds, and write it on their hearts; and I will be their God, and they shall be My people. No more shall every man teach his neighbor, and every man his brother, saying, "Know the LORD," for they all shall know Me, from the least of them to the greatest of them, says the LORD. For I will forgive their

iniquity, and their sin I will remember no more (Jeremiah 31:33-34).

Everyone should realize that the coming 1000-year kingdom will be the most incredible era ever in earth's history. It will be a time of unprecedented peace, when those who have accepted Jesus Christ as their Lord and Savior will reign alongside their loving King. It will most certainly be a time best described by the word *utopia*. For in that day, "they shall beat their swords into plowshares, and their spears into pruning hooks; nation shall not lift up sword against nation, neither shall they learn war anymore" (Isaiah 2:4).

Such world peace is beyond finite human comprehension. Despite the fact that the words of Isaiah 2:4 are etched on the United Nations building in New York, there is no way depraved humanity will ever be able to bring about such conditions on earth. But, thank God, such will be reality when Jesus returns to reign on the earth.

A Wondrous Age

Ever since the fall of Adam and Eve in the Garden of Eden, humanity and creation have been under the judgment and ramifications of their original sin. The pollution of sin has affected all of humanity and all of creation. The apostle Paul reminds us of that which we experience daily when he declares in Romans 8:22, "We know that the whole creation has been groaning as in the pains of childbirth right up to the present time" (NIV). However, during the millennial kingdom there will be a partial lifting of the curse and ramifications of original sin. There will still be death (for those who entered the millennium in their natural bodies), and the complete effects of the fall will not be lifted until the creation of the new heaven and new earth in the eternal state after the millennium (Revelation 22:3).

The coming literal kingdom of Christ to this earth will be the most blessed time this world has known since the Garden of Eden.

In fact, many Edenic features will characterize it. All those who rebelled against God will be gone. Satan will be bound literally so he cannot tempt man, and Christ will enforce righteousness. Of course, this righteousness will be enforced with the help of His holy angels and the church. No doubt it will be illegal for pornographers, criminals, and others who traditionally corrupt society to ply their evil trades.

The coming kingdom will be a time of unprecedented prosperity, when everyone will have his own home. The curse on the earth will be lifted and the ground will bear incredible harvests. Cheating and war will be nonexistent, so people will be able to enjoy the fruits of their labors.

Isaiah 65 indicates that longevity will be increased to almost what it was prior to the flood, when people lived to almost 1000 years of age. At least that will be the case for believers, who will live from the time of their birth until the end of the kingdom. Isaiah 65:20 indicates that a person will be considered still a child at 100 years of age.

Note carefully what the last half of Isaiah 65:20 says: "The child shall die one hundred years old, but the sinner being one hundred years old shall be accursed." Evidently God will allow that all people be permitted at least 100 years of life in the most ideal environment since the Garden of Eden so that they can put their faith in Jesus Christ. Yet sad to say, even then some people won't. That's why Isaiah declares that "the sinner being one hundred years old shall be accursed"—which means "cut off." That God would give 100 years for people to make the decision to accept Christ as Savior is an incredible expression of His love, mercy, longsuffering, and forgiveness (Exodus 34:6). This affirms Peter's statement, "The Lord is…not willing that any should perish but that all should come to repentance" (2 Peter 3:9).

Not only will lifespans be considerably longer, but the world population will be enormous. Jeremiah 33:22 speaks of this when it says, "As the host of heaven cannot be numbered, nor the sand of the sea measured, so will I multiply the descendants of David. My servant and the Levites who minister to Me." In Zechariah 8:5, we read that "the streets of the city shall be full of boys and girls," indicating that the population in Israel will increase dramatically. Keep in mind that we will live under ideal conditions in the millennial kingdom—there will be no wars to wipe out large numbers of people, and we will not experience the level of violence seen either now or during the Tribulation period.

A Time of Faith

The millennial kingdom will be a time of faith, when the majority of the world's population will be believers. Christ will be in charge, so there won't be immoral or other forms of media programming available to blind people's minds to the gospel. Body-damaging substances will not be available, so people will not have their minds fogged from the truths of Scripture; Satan will be bound so he cannot blind them spiritually. Even art forms will glorify Christ during the millennial kingdom. Jeremiah 31:31-34 indicates that everyone will be so acquainted with the gospel that no one will need to share it with his neighbor.

The government and politics of the millennial kingdom will focus on the benevolent reign of Jesus Christ as Israel's Messiah-King. It will be a theocracy centered in Jerusalem (Isaiah 2:1-4), where Jesus will reign as both Messiah and King of Israel, thus fulfilling God's prophetic promise to King David in the Davidic Covenant (2 Samuel 7:12-16). God's covenant with David guaranteed David's dynasty, throne, and kingdom would continue forever. When Jesus Christ returns at the end of the Tribulation, He will reestablish the Davidic throne in His personal rule (Jeremiah 23:5-8). Other significant passages describing Christ's reign over Israel include Psalm 2, Isaiah 9:6-7, Jeremiah 33:20-26, Ezekiel 34:23-25 and 37:23-24, and Luke 1:32-33. These and other passages provide ample specific evidence that the kingdom promised to David will be fully realized in the future.

The Final Rebellion

But in spite of all the ideal conditions arranged by God to attract a maximum number of people to accept His free gift of salvation by receiving His Son, many will rebel at the end of the millennial kingdom. Revelation 20:8 says that at the end of this 1000-year era, Satan will be let loose from the bottomless pit to go out "to deceive the nations"—that is, to tempt them to rebel against God. The reason God allows this to happen is so that all the unsaved people living on the earth will be forced to make a decision about whether they will receive Christ before God establishes the eternal order.

What's sad is that even after living for so many years under the righteous reign of Christ, there will still be a multitude "whose number is as the sand of the sea" (Revelation 20:8) who will rebel against God when given the opportunity. Among other things, this suggests that it isn't entirely Satan's fault that people reject Christ, but rather, people rebel by their own will. Satan's appearance on the scene at this point will simply bring to the surface the rebellion within the hearts of those who "are not willing to come" to Him that they might have eternal life (John 5:40).

The End of Satan

Satan's one last attempt to lash out against God will end in failure. Revelation 20:10 says, "The devil, who deceived them, was cast into the lake of fire and brimstone where the beast and the false prophet are. And they will be tormented day and night forever and ever." The ability of living creatures to suffer indefinitely in the lake of fire is seen in the fact that the beast (or Antichrist) and the false prophet are men. They are thrown into the lake of fire at the beginning of the 1000-year kingdom (Revelation 19:20), yet they are spoken of in the present tense in Revelation 20:10, indicating that they are still there. It is into this lake of fire that Satan will be cast. He, the Antichrist, the false prophet, and all those from every age in history who rejected God's free offer of salvation through faith in Christ will "be tormented day and night forever and ever." The Bible clearly states, then, that this punishment will last for all eternity!

CHAPTER 12

The New Jerusalem

As the Book of the Revelation comes to a close, we come to the very end of time and the beginning of eternity future. All of God's judgments have finally come to completion. All of the nations have come to stand before the Lord Himself. The saved have entered into heaven. The lost have been cast into the Lake of Fire. Then, in the final two chapters in the Bible, the revelator John looks into the distant future and sees the new heaven, the new earth, and the New Jerusalem: "I saw a new heaven and a new earth, for the first heaven and the first earth had passed away. Also there was no more sea" (Revelation 21:1).

People debate, "Will the new heaven be a reconstitution of the old heaven and earth, or will it be something brand new?" Consider this for starters: If there is no ocean, there is no plankton. That alone is a very big clue about how different things will be. The environment will not sustain life the same way it does on Planet Earth today. This implies that the new earth is a whole new place.

Then John says, "I...saw the holy city, New Jerusalem, coming down out of heaven from God, prepared as a bride adorned for her

155

husband" (Revelation 21:2). This is a picture of the ultimate dwelling place of the bride of Christ, the heavenly city, the city that ultimately will be all that God ever intended the earthly Jerusalem to be. But it will be far better and far greater than anything that we could ever imagine.

John continues: "I heard a loud voice from heaven saying, Behold, the tabernacle of God is with men, and He will dwell with them, and they shall be his people. God Himself will be with them and be their God" (Revelation 21:3). The promise in this passage is for every saved person who has ever lived. Old Testament saints, church age saints, Tribulation saints, millennial saints—all the people of God for all the ages of time—are there in the family of God in the eternal city. Here the bride of Christ is the great new city of Jerusalem itself.

Revelation 21:4-5 then says,

> God will wipe away every tear from their eyes; there shall
> be no more death, nor sorrow, nor crying. There shall be
> no more pain, for the former things have passed away.
> Then He who sat on the throne said, "Behold, I make all
> things new." And He said to me, "Write, for these words
> are true and faithful."

This is the new eternity: the new heaven, the new earth, the New Jerusalem, the ultimate experience of the people of God. John spends two whole chapters describing this place to us so that we can have a sneak preview of what it is like. The water of life is there. The tree of life is there. The blessing of God is there. And best of all, God is there. In verse 11, we learn that the glory of God lights the city. It is resplendent with the glory of God Himself. In fact, John goes on to say there is no need of the sun or the moon to light this city, for the glory of God illuminates it (Revelation 21:23).

Think of what that means in a biblical sense. In the Old Testament, the glory of God, the Shekinah glory, resided on the Ark of the Covenant. Only the high priest could enter the Holy of Holies and stand in the presence of God's glory. Remember what happened when Moses saw the reflected glory of God? God said to him, "I cannot look at you face to face. You will not be able to live if you stand in My presence" (see Exodus 33:20). And the reflected glory of God glowed on the face of Moses.

God will live in our midst in the eternal city, in the New Jerusalem. Revelation 22:4 says, "And they shall see his face." What a promise! There, in the presence of God, you will become a priest of God, a king with Christ, and reign with Him through all eternity. The promise of Scripture is that Jesus rules in our hearts now, in the church age. Then Jesus will rule on earth during the millennial kingdom. But in eternity, we will rule with Him forever and ever over the whole universe. Imagine what an honor and privilege that will be!

Some of the nearest stars in outer space are many light-years away from us. Even in today's space vehicles you would not be able to reach them in the course of a lifetime. But in eternity, you will have countless ages to explore the vast universe. You will have endless opportunities to discover new worlds, new places, and new things.

The description of the Holy City of New Jerusalem is one of the most amazing passages in one of the greatest prophecies in the Bible. Look again in Revelation chapter 21. Notice that verse 12 says the heavenly city will have a great high wall and 12 gates. At the gates will be 12 angels, and on the gates will be the names of the 12 tribes of the children of Israel.

Then we read in verse 14 that the city will have a wall with 12 foundations, and these foundations are named for the 12 apostles of the Lord Jesus. In other words, the heavenly city will encompass the entire family of God. It is for both saved Jews and Gentiles. It is for those who knew the Lord in the Old Testament dispensation, and those who know the Lord in the New Testament dispensation. The gates of the city are named for the 12 tribes of Israel and the foundations are named for the 12 apostles. All of this reminds us that the entire family of God will be there for all eternity.

Biblically speaking, 12 seems to be a number with governmental or administrative significance. In Scripture we see multiples of 12 in the administration of God's universe. These include, for example, the 24 thrones in Revelation 4:4, as well as the 144,000 Christians in Revelation 14, who will probably hold special leadership positions during the millennial kingdom. Additional references to 12 are mentioned in the description of the New Jerusalem in Revelation 21:9-21:

Twelve gates. Twelve entrances will always be open for God's people to have access to the New Jerusalem. Revelation 21:13 indicates there will be three gates on each of the four sides of this gigantic city. The names of the 12 tribes of Israel will be inscribed on the gates.

Twelve angels. Again we see the relationship of angels in the eternal order and their work with the human race.

Twelve tribes. These indicate that the children of Israel will have ready access to this splendid heavenly city. Since angels are mentioned, it seems that each of the tribes has its angel, just as each of the churches has its angel (see Revelation chapters 2 and 3).

Twelve foundations. The foundation walls of the city will be magnificent beyond comprehension. In Revelation 21:19-21 they are described as "adorned with all kinds of precious stones."

Then John says in verse 16 that the city "is laid out as a square." It is as wide as it is long as it is high. It is like a gigantic cube 1500 miles wide and high and deep. It would quite easily accommodate the billions of people who have come to know Christ as their personal Savior over the centuries. All of the family of God will live there: Old Testament saints, New testament believers, Tribulation and millennial saints.

Then John tries again to describe the indescribable. He speaks of precious stones and lists and names all of those stones, many of which were found on the breastplate of the High Priest of Israel. Those stones then symbolize this great city that is coming in the future. Then John says in verse 22, "I saw no temple in it, for the

Lord God Almighty and the Lamb are its temple." John's description reveals these details about the city:

1. Splendor: like a jasper, clear as crystal (Revelation 21:11)

2. Wall: 144 cubits (220 feet) high (verse 17)

3. Gates: giant pearls, named for the 12 tribes of Israel (verses 12,21)

4. Measurement: foursquare, or 1500-mile cube (verse 16)

5. City itself: pure gold, like clear glass (verse 18)

6. Street: pure gold, like transparent glass (verse 21)

7. Temple: God and the Lamb are the temple (verse 22)

8. Light: glory of God and the Lamb (verse 23)

9. Nations: those who are saved (verse 24)

10. Access: gates that are never closed (verse 25)

11. Activity: no night there (verse 25)

12. Purity: none who defile are present (verse 27)

The Heavenly Temple

If this is the Holy City, then where is the heavenly temple? The heavenly temple is the pattern in heaven of the earthly temple down below. But in Revelation 21, John describes the heavenly temple in a totally different way: "I saw no temple in it, for the Lord God Almighty and the Lamb are its temple" (verse 22).

In other words, God Himself is the temple. We will dwell there with Him and in Him in His presence. The earthly temple kept the high priest out of the Holy of Holies except on the Day of Atonement, kept the other priests limited to the Holy Place, and kept the laymen limited to the courtyard. By contrast, in heaven, no one will be limited. Everybody will have access into the presence of God Himself. That is the holy temple of the New Jerusalem.

Revelation 21:23 further states that "the city had no need of the sun or of the moon to shine in it, for the glory of God illuminated it. The Lamb is its light." In these closing words in the book of Revelation, we see that the Son is coequal with the Father. The emphasis in these passages is on the deity of Christ.

Verse 24 then tells us who will be present with the Father and the Son: "The nations of those who are saved shall walk in its light, and the kings of the earth bring their glory and honor into it." Only the saved will enter into the New Jerusalem. Only those who belong to God will be in the new heaven and the new earth. Only they will participate in the family of God for all eternity.

Then John tells us who is not going to be there. In verse 27 he says, "There shall by no means enter it anything that defiles, or causes an abomination or a lie, but only those who are written in the Lamb's Book of Life." That is, those who were never saved, whose hearts were never transformed, whose eternal destiny was never changed will not be there.

The good news is that anyone who wants to come into the presence of God in heaven may come. The final invitation of the Scripture is "Let him who thirsts come. Whoever desires, let him take the water of life freely" (Revelation 22:17). But those who do not choose to come, who do not put their faith and trust in Christ, will be excluded. They will not be there.

The saved of the nations will dwell in heaven for all eternity. This is God's promise to every believer, to every person whose name is written in the Lamb's book of life.

In the opening of Revelation chapter 22, John continues, "He showed me a pure river of water of life, clear as crystal, proceeding from the throne of God and of the Lamb...and on either side of the river, was the tree of life." The tree of life has not appeared in the Bible since Genesis 3, when Adam and Eve were banished from the Garden of Eden. The tree of life is the symbol that paradise is regained in the heavenly city, in the heavenly temple. There, the people of God will have access to the presence of God, the life of God, and the power of God.

The Promise of Eternal Life

Jesus promised His followers, "Because I live, you will live also" (John 14:19). Not surprisingly, no one in the Bible speaks more about the resurrection than Jesus Christ Himself. In John 11:25-26, for example, He said, "I am the resurrection and the life. He who believes in Me, though he may die, he shall live. And whoever lives and believes in Me shall never die." Jesus was saying that although those who believe in Him may die physically, the real person, which is the soul and spirit, will never die.

In John 5:24-29, Christ taught,

> Most assuredly, I say to you, he who hears My word and believes in Him who sent Me has everlasting life, and shall not come into judgment, but has passed from death into life. Most assuredly, I say to you, the hour is coming, and now is, when the dead will hear the voice of the Son of God; and those who hear will live. For as the Father has life in Himself, so He has granted the Son to have life in Himself, and has given Him authority to execute judgment also, because He is the Son of Man. Do not marvel at this; for the hour is coming in which all who are in the graves will hear His voice and come forth—those who have done good, to the resurrection of life, and those who have done evil, to the resurrection of condemnation.

From the above passage, we know that both the righteous and unrighteous will be resurrected. Eternal life is therefore guaranteed for all. However, where and how that eternal life will play out depends entirely on one's position in Christ.

Our Eternal Destiny

Prior to the death, burial, and resurrection of Jesus Christ, all people who died were taken to a place known as Sheol or Hades. Bible scholars have long speculated about where this might be, and the Bible doesn't tell us. Based on Luke 16:26, it appears this place had two compartments separated by a large chasm or gulf. The first section was known as paradise or the place of comfort. This is where the Old Testament saints would go following death. On the other side of the great gulf was the place of torment, where those who died without faith were held. Ever since Jesus' resurrection, believers have no longer gone to the place of comfort in Sheol, but rather, have been instantly transported to heaven to be with the Lord (see 2 Corinthians 5:8). Unbelievers, on the other hand, are still taken to the "place of torment" in Sheol/Hades.

The word *heaven* appears nearly 600 times in the Bible. It can refer to three different places: 1) the atmospheric heaven or sky; 2) the planetary heaven where the sun, moon, and stars reside; or 3) the third heaven, which Paul speaks of in 2 Corinthians 12, where God dwells with His angels and His people. This is where believers who have died are today. Everything that is truly precious to us as Christians will be in this third heaven, including the triune God, our loved ones who are believers, our inheritance, our citizenship, and our eternal rewards. In other words, everything of eternal value will be there.

When the rapture occurs, we who are believers will instantly receive our new, immortal, resurrected bodies, and Christ will take us home to the Father's house in heaven (John 14:1-4). Many of us look forward to that glorious day when we will see the unfathomable magnificence of heaven, be reunited with loved ones, and come face-to-face with Jesus, our Savior. What some of us fail to realize, however, is that immediately following the rapture, we will stand before the judgment seat of Christ and receive rewards, if any, for the good works we performed in the name of Christ during our time on earth. Then, while still in heaven, we will participate in the marriage supper of the Lamb, at which we will become the bride of Christ (Revelation 19:7-9). Finally, at the conclusion of the Tribulation (which will take place while we believers are in heaven), we will return with Jesus to earth and rule with Him during the 1000-year kingdom (Revelation 20:1-3).

At the time of the rapture, the bodies of those who happen to be alive on earth at the time, along with the bodies of believers who have already died, will be changed from corruptible into incorruptible (see 1 Corinthians 15:52-54). Presently, our bodies are unfit for heaven and must be transformed into bodies similar to Christ's resurrection body. These new, resurrected bodies (made from the elements of our old bodies gathered together by the Lord) will be recognizable, able to communicate, and able to eat, just as Jesus ate with His disciples after His resurrection (see Luke 24:41-43; John 21:9-14). Jesus also demonstrated that He could walk through walls and travel great distances at the speed of thought in His resurrected body. It's very likely that we will be able to do the same.

Eternal Punishment of the Lost

Contrasting sharply with the glorious future that awaits each and every believer is the fate of the unbeliever, which is simply too horrifying to even imagine. As mentioned earlier, at the moment of death, the unbeliever is instantly taken to the place of torment in hell (Greek, *hades*). According to Revelation 20:11-15, at the conclusion of the millennial kingdom, unbelievers will be resurrected and brought out of Sheol/Hades to stand before Jesus Christ at the Great White Throne Judgment. There, they will be judged "according to their works" (verse 12) using the Law of the Old Testament. Because none of them ever became born again, and because their names were removed from the Book of Life, none will be able to enter the kingdom of God. All these unbelievers will then be cast into the Lake of Fire, where they will be tormented for all eternity.

Had they accepted Christ's free gift of salvation while they were alive on earth, they would not have had to be punished with eternal separation from God.

The term "lake of fire" appears five times in Revelation (19:20; 20:10,14-15; 21:8). It is a place of conscious punishment. At present, no one is in the Lake of Fire. Its first occupants will be the Beast and the false prophet (Revelation 19:20). When unbelievers die today, they go immediately to hell (hades) to await their final trial at the Great White Throne Judgment. After that they will be condemned to the Lake of Fire for all eternity. They will experience what is called the "second death" (Revelation 21:8). The first death is physical death, whereas the second involves eternal punishment.

Hell is most definitely a place of torment and punishment. But it serves only as a holding place for those awaiting God's final judgment. By contrast, the Lake of Fire is a place of permanent incarceration from which there is no release. In the New Testament, this place serves as a symbol of eternal punishment (see Matthew 25:41-46; Mark 9:44-48).

No Option for Limbo, Purgatory, Annihilation, or Reincarnation

Despite the teachings of many in today's world, we must understand that God's Word clearly does not allow for other options regarding the afterlife. Purgatory is said to be the place where people go to do penance or suffer for the sins they have committed in this world in order to purify them for a better afterlife. The startling difference between the biblical presentation of the present state of the dead and this false teaching is that there is no indication whatsoever in the Bible that those in the torment section of Sheol/Hades or those in heaven will ever be anywhere but where they are for all eternity. Luke 16:26 makes clear that anyone who goes to the place of torment can never bridge the great gulf fixed and enter Paradise.

On the contrary, all those who are presently in torment will eventually be cast into the Lake of Fire.

The suggestion that those in torment today will be granted a later opportunity to be saved contradicts Isaiah 38:18, which says, "Sheol cannot thank You, death cannot praise You; those who go down to the pit cannot hope for Your truth." The place of torment is essentially a place of suffering and is void of the teaching of truth. Therefore those who enter that place cannot hope for escape. This is a tragic truth, and we dare not diminish its reality in any way.

Highest Heaven

The New Jerusalem is described in the Bible as the highest heaven. The apostle Paul said in 2 Corinthians 12:2 that he was "caught up to the third heaven." He was not referring to the atmosphere around our planet, the clouds, or outer space, but to the dwelling place of God. That is the place being described for us here in Revelation chapters 21–22.

Though we don't know a lot about our future dwelling place, one of the more important things we do know is this: "There shall be no more curse" (22:3). The curse of sin will be gone. It will be removed forever, never to afflict us again.

And "the throne of God and of the Lamb shall be in it, and His servants shall serve Him. They shall see his face" (Revelation 22:3-4). At the time this was written, the phrase "they shall see his face" was an idiom that referred to a person having an audience with a king. The average person never saw a king face-to-face. If you had an audience with the king, you had an opportunity to look right into his face. What John is saying here is that in heaven, we will have an audience with the King on a regular basis. And we will enjoy this privilege for all of eternity!

In that passage, John also states that we are going to be God's servants. We will serve Him forever. We will not become bored because there's nothing to do. We will stay busy serving the Lord. And verse 5 adds that along with serving, we will "reign forever and ever." We will serve the Lord and rule with Him over the vast expanse of the universe. And that's just a glimpse of all that awaits us!

Ultimately, we are going to see it all. We are not going to need a rocket of any source to get us from one universe to another, from one experience to another. No, we will have time and opportunity to do it all, to see it all, and to experience it all.

So many of us live with the mentality, "I need to travel and see the world while I have a chance." People have their "bucket list" of the 1001 things they want to do before they die. Well, there will be millions of things for you to do for all eternity, where you will not die. That is the promise of the Bible: You will serve the Lord forever, and you will reign with Him forever. What a promise!

Then as John wraps up the book of Revelation, he pens these words from Jesus:

> I am Alpha and Omega, the Beginning and the End, the First and the Last. Blessed are those who do his commandments, that they may have right to the tree of life, and may enter in through the gates into the city (Revelation 22:13-14).

We who live in heaven will be blessed. We'll have access to the tree of life and to God's throne. We're going to experience blessing upon blessing upon blessing. Every good thing that comes from God's hand will be made known to us.

Then John closes with an instruction and an invitation, both of which come from Jesus Himself:

> "I, Jesus, have sent My angel to testify to you these things in the churches. I am the Root and the Offspring of David, the Bright and Morning Star." And the Spirit and the bride say, "Come!" And let him who hears say,

"Come!" And let him who thirsts come. Whoever desires, let him take the water of life freely (verses 16-17).

Christ personally commands that these truths are to be communicated to the churches. That is, prophecy is an important part of the church's teachings. Then He gives one final invitation that people would receive Him as their Savior. Our prayer is that you have accepted this invitation and that you too are a child of God. For if you are, then you will experience all the incredible wonders of heaven that we've reviewed in this chapter.

We who have salvation in Christ have a grand future ahead of us. We have a lot to look forward to. This should cause us to live in great anticipation of Jesus' return. And so it is with that in mind that we close this book in hearty agreement with the apostle John's emphatic declaration in verse 20: "Even so, come, Lord Jesus!"

A Final Word

The Bible tells us we can know that we have eternal life (1 John 5:13). With absolute certainty, you can know that Jesus died on the cross, that He rose from the dead, and that He is coming again. You can know whether or not you have said yes to Him. Going to heaven is not a matter of guesswork. It is not a matter of saying, "I hope I'm going to make it. I think I've done the right thing." No, Jesus did the right thing when He went to the cross and died in your place, when He took the wrath of God against you on Himself, and when He rose from the dead to make it possible for you to receive the gift of eternal life. All we need to do is to put our faith and trust in what He did. The Bible is telling us the truth when it says that whoever will call on the name of the Lord will be saved (Romans 10:13).

You can know that you are ready to meet the Lord because you have made the decision to put your faith and trust in Him. And if you want to make that decision today, we urge you to call on Him right now. You might want to pray something like this sincerely from your heart:

God, I know that I need a Savior. I know I need Your forgiveness. And I really do believe that Jesus died in my place, that He rose again, and that He is coming again. I want to know for sure that He is coming for me. And today, I am committing my heart, life, and soul to Him by faith.

If you are making that decision for the very first time today, please write or go online and let us know of your decision. We would like to send you some material that will help you as you begin your new walk with Christ.

www.timlahaye.com

or

www.thekingiscoming.com

Appendixes

Key Events in the History of Modern Israel

In the more than 60 years since Israel has been rebirthed as a nation, many key events have taken place. Some of them are noted here in addition to those provided within the chapters of this book.

May 14, 1948—The United Nations officially recognized the State of Israel. US president Harry Truman wrote a letter of recognition in support of this. The Israeli government established the State of Israel, thus fulfilling the 2500-year-old prophecy recorded in Ezekiel 37. Great Britain ended its mandate in Palestine and removed its troops, leaving behind some 650,000 Jews to govern themselves. This turn of events was unacceptable to the Arab world. Egypt, Syria, Saudi Arabia, Lebanon, and Iraq united together and immediately declared war on Israel within hours following the declaration of sovereignty. The Arab armies easily outnumbered the Israelis, and although thousands of Jews died in the ensuing combat, Israel miraculously was able to defeat its Arab neighbors. Some 350,000 additional Arabs who refused to recognize the State of Israel fled to neighboring Arab countries such as Lebanon, Syria, Iraq, and Saudi Arabia.

1956—Egypt, under the direction of Gamel Abdel Nasser, tried to nationalize the Suez Canal following British withdrawal from the area. Israel invaded the Sinai Peninsula and in eight days reached the canal, gaining control over the northernmost point of the Gulf of Aqaba. Nasser suffered a military defeat but gained an eventual political victory by retaining control of the Suez Canal.

1964—The Palestinian Liberation organization (PLO) was founded by Palestinian Arabs in order to create an armed force capable of coercing Israel to give up land that could be used for an independent Arab-controlled Palestine. The move led to inflamed Palestinian nationalism that would result in a series of wars and conflicts which continue to this very day.

1967—Six-Day War. The Israeli intelligence agency, Mossad, uncovered Arab plans to launch an immediate military attack against Israel. Mossad also discovered that Russia was in the process of supplying large shipments of arms to the Arab countries that were planning this attack. Rather than waiting for the Arab assault, Israel launched predawn land and air strikes against Egypt, Jordan, and Syria. Although outnumbered 30 to 1, Israel was able to quickly destroy the Egyptian air force and navy as well as overcome Syria from the air. Israel's tanks reached the Suez Canal and decisively captured Soviet-built missile bases intact.

The war lasted less than a week, hence the name the Six-Day War. With its stunning military victory, Israel controlled the Sinai Peninsula, the West Bank, and the Golan Heights. This more than quadrupled Israel's territory from 8000 to 34,000 square miles. For the first time since the Roman era, the city of Jerusalem was under Jewish control. However, within a few days of the victory, Israeli defense minister Moshe Dayan, meeting with Muslim leaders at the al-Aqsa Mosque, inexplicably returned administrative control of the Temple Mount site over to the Palestinians, declaring Jerusalem to be an international city.

1973—Syria and Egypt attacked Israel while Jews were in their synagogues observing Yom Kippur, the Day of Atonement. The three-week-long Yom Kippur War began. This was the final time the Israeli military found itself unready in the face of an attack. Once again, the Arabs, equipped with Russian-supplied armaments, attacked Israel in multiple simultaneous operations. Egypt seized large portions of the Sinai, while Syria took the Golan Heights. Israel, however, was able to break through enemy lines and cross the Suez Canal, thereby cutting off the advancing Egyptian army. At the same time, Israel retook the Golan Heights, forged into Syria, and was about to conquer Damascus, but was stopped in its tracks by a UN-enforced cease-fire. As with previous wars, Israel won this one as well, but suffered tremendous casualties.

1978—At a conference hosted by US president Jimmy Carter at Camp David in Maryland, President Sadat of Egypt and Prime Minister Menachem Begin of Israel signed agreements known as the Camp David Accords. This led to the signing of a formal peace treaty between the two countries on March 26, 1979. In keeping with this agreement, Israel officially withdrew its troops from the city of El Arish and returned Sinai to Egyptian control.

1981—In a daring early-morning raid on Baghdad, 600 miles north of their air base, eight Israeli F-16 fighters with six F-15s flying cover, destroyed a French-built nuclear generator in Iraq. Israel believed that Iraq was planning to utilize the plutonium generator to build atomic weapons for use against Israel. Formally, the world was outraged by Israel's actions, but secretly many world leaders were relieved that the hostile and unpredictable Iraq would not become a nuclear power.

1981—President Sadat of Egypt was assassinated on October 6 while watching a military parade. The incident was traced to Arab terrorists opposed to Sadat's friendly attitude toward Israel. Hosni Mubarak, Sadat's eventual successor, subsequently opened Egypt's borders to Libya but maintained the official peace treaty with Israel.

1983—A truck bomb blew up at the US Marine compound at the Beirut, Lebanon airport, killing 241 US servicemen who were part of a peace-keeping force. A similar attack at the French compound killed an additional 58 soldiers, shattering confidence in a lasting peace in the region.

1984—8000 Jews were secretly rescued from Ethiopia and taken safely to Israel as part of an effort called Operation Moses. During the 1980s and 1990s, thousands of Jews were taken to Israel from Iraq, Iran, and nations that were formerly part of the Soviet Union.

1987—On December 6, an Israeli was stabbed to death while shopping in Gaza. The next day, four residents of the Jabalia refugee camp in Gaza were killed in a traffic accident. False rumors began spreading among the

Palestinians that the four accident victims had been killed by Israelis out of revenge. Mass rioting broke out two days later and spread across the West Bank, Gaza, and Jerusalem in what would become known as the Intifada. The violence, orchestrated by the PLO and directed toward both Israeli soldiers and civilians alike, continued for the next several years. During this time 27 Israelis were killed and more than 3100 injured. The PLO-dominated Unified Leadership of the Intifada issued leaflets dictating on which days violence was to be escalated and who was to be its target. Methods of violence included the throwing of Molotov cocktails and hand grenades, shootings, stabbings, bombings, and burnings with acid. The PLO also used the occasion to execute Palestinians whom they believed had "associations" with the Israelis.

1990—On August 2, Saddam Hussein of Iraq invaded Kuwait. Four days later, the UN Security Council imposed economic sanctions against Iraq. The next day, the US began sending troops into the Persian Gulf area. Hussein announced that any military action taken against Iraq would result in a strike on Israel. Iraqi foreign minister Tariq Aziz threatened that Iraq would use chemical weapons if Israel decided to strike back. On December 23, Saddam Hussein announced that Tel Aviv would be Iraq's first target if invaded.

1991—The Gulf War began on January 15. Over the next five weeks, 38 SCUD missiles were launched at Israel from Iraq, resulting in one fatality and 172 injuries. On February 28, the Gulf War ended with the expulsion of the Iraqi army from Kuwait by the US and coalition forces.

1993—Israel secretly signed a peace agreement with the PLO in Oslo, Norway, on August 20. Several days later both groups signed letters formally recognizing each other's right to exist. On September 13, the historic handshake took place between Israel's prime minister Yitzhak Rabin and PLO leader Yasser Arafat. On September 23, the Israeli Knesset ratified the Oslo Agreement by a vote of 61 to 50, with 8 abstentions. One year later, Rabin and Arafat were awarded the Nobel Peace Prize.

1995—Israeli Prime Minister Yitzhak Rabin was assassinated at a peace rally by a Jewish extremist. Heads of state from all over the world, including Jordan's King Hussein and President Mubarak of Egypt, attended Rabin's funeral in Jerusalem. Yigal Amir was later indicted for the murder. The future of the Israeli-PLO negotiations was now in doubt.

1996—Jerusalem celebrated its 3000th anniversary as the capital of the Jewish state, dating back to King David's conquest of the city in biblical times. Later that year, newly elected Israeli prime minister Benjamin Netanyahu announced the opening of a new archaeological tunnel alongside the Western Wall in Jerusalem, triggering a deadly series of Palestinian protests resulting in 14 Israeli and 56 Palestinian deaths.

1998—The US embassies in Nairobi, Kenya and Dar es Salaam, Tanzania were simultaneously bombed by al-Qaeda terrorists, resulting in 224 dead and more than 4000 wounded. Islamic terrorist leader Osama bin Laden was later confirmed to be the mastermind behind the massacres. The Israeli Defense Force aided in the rescue efforts in Nairobi. Later that same year, Netanyahu and Arafat signed the Wye River Memorandum to redeploy portions of the West Bank and Gaza Strip. This was done at the White House in the presence of US president Bill Clinton and King Hussein of Jordan.

2000—US President Bill Clinton attempted to negotiate a peace treaty between Israeli prime minister Ehud Barak and Palestinian president Yasser Arafat. Barak agreed to the treaty's terms but Arafat refused, making it painfully obvious that the Palestinians really did not want peace with Israel.

September 11, 2001—Islamic terrorists sponsored by al-Qaeda hijacked and crashed jetliners into the twin towers of the World Trade Center in New York and the Pentagon in Washington, DC. Nearly 3000 people were killed. Thousands of Palestinians and other Muslims celebrated in the streets while the rest of the world mourned and expressed outrage. The US retaliated by invading al-Qaeda-dominated Afghanistan and setting up a democratically elected government in the Islamic nation.

2002—Israel erected a security force along the West Bank to help prevent future terrorist infiltrations into Israel. Israeli prime minister Ariel Sharon met with US president George W. Bush, who proposed a peace plan known as the Road Map, which called for the creation of a permanent Palestinian state.

2005—Mahmoud Abbas was elected the new president of the Palestinian Authority, replacing Yasser Arafat, who had died two months earlier in Paris, France. Early in 2006, Ariel Sharon suffered a severe stroke and was replaced by Ehud Olmert.

2006—After a series of air and missile attacks between Israel and Hezbollah in Lebanon, Iranian president Mahmoud Ahmadinejad announced that Israel will one day be "wiped out" just as the Soviet Union was, drawing applause from participants in a Holocaust-denying rally in Tehran.

2007—Israeli Air Force destroys a suspected nuclear reactor in Syria built with assistance from North Korea.

2008—Large-scale conflict in Gaza in response to ongoing rocket fire in the western Negev.

2010—The Free Gaza Movement sends flotilla that are stopped by Israeli naval forces. These events served as part of the larger blockade of Gaza. Nine activists were killed on board one flotilla. Several flotilla passengers and Israeli soldiers were wounded.

2011—Israeli embassy attacked in Cairo by a reported 3000 Egyptian protesters.

2012—Operation Pillar of Defense took place, during which numerous Hamas targets were attacked in Gaza in response to ongoing rocket fire in the western Negev.

2014—After Hamas and other Palestinian militant groups had fired 4500-plus rockets at Israel from Gaza, Israel launched what was called Operation Protective Edge. This involved targeted air strikes and the destruction of Hamas tunnels that led underground into Israel. A twelfth cease-fire tentatively helds after 50 days of destruction. The first 11 cease-fire agreements were all broken by Hamas in Gaza. The situation remains tense, although Israel destroyed numerous concrete tunnels that had been built by Hamas to potentially invade Israel.

We can readily see from this list of significant events that the modern State of Israel is in a very unique and precarious position. It is obvious that God is doing a special work. Nearly 2000 years went by before the Jewish people once again had a nation to call their own. The prophet Isaiah asked: "Can a nation be born in a day?" (see Isaiah 66:8). In the case of Israel, the answer is a resounding yes!

The significance of Israel's reemergence in her ancient homeland is that this had to occur in order to set the stage for the fulfillment of biblical prophecies about the last days. Israel must be a nation in her own land in order for the end times to come about. Incredible as it sounds, the existence of Israel today is the number one evidence that God is continuing to fulfill Bible prophecy in a literal manner. God said Israel would one day regather, and it has come to pass—to His glory and honor.

Frequently Asked Questions About Israel and the End Times

If an unbeliever hears, understands, and rejects the gospel before the Tribulation, would he or she be able to become saved during the Tribulation?

We believe that unbelievers will still have the opportunity to become saved during the Tribulation regardless of how much they have been exposed to the gospel before the rapture.

Those who argue that unbelievers who reject the gospel before the rapture will not be able to become saved during the Tribulation base their logic on 2 Thessalonians 2:10-12:

> ...with all unrighteous deception among those who perish, because they did not receive the love of the truth, that they might be saved. And for this reason God will send them strong delusion, that they should believe the lie, that they all may be condemned who did not believe the truth but had pleasure in unrighteousness.

Proponents of this view contend that God, through the Antichrist, will actively delude those who do not believe. While this is true, nothing in the passage suggests that the delusion is the result of an individual's unbelief and rejection of the gospel prior to the rapture. There are a number of reasons we believe that 2 Thessalonians 2:10-12 does not support this view.

First, 2 Thessalonians 2 does not say anything about an individual hearing, understanding, and then rejecting the gospel. It does make a universal statement about those who do not love the truth. Thus, all unbelievers are referred to in the same way as one group. There is no basis in this passage for thinking that there is any kind of a subclass of unbelievers made up of those who heard the gospel, understood it, and rejected it.

Second, the context of the entire passage relates to what will happen during the forthcoming Tribulation period. The context for when "they did not receive the love of the truth" (verse 10) is the Tribulation. So 2 Thessalonians 2 is talking about the response of unbelievers during the Tribulation.

If the passage were referring to an unbelieving response prior to the Tribulation, with a result that such a decision would impact one's destiny during the Tribulation, then the passage would probably have been worded differently in order to convey such a message. Since it is not so configured, there is no support for such.

Specific support that verses 8-12 involve events that will transpire during the Tribulation starts in verse 8, which begins, "And then the lawless one will be revealed..." In other words, "then" denotes a shift from the current church age into a future era, the Tribulation. Nothing in verses 8-12 takes any part of that passage out of the context of the Tribulation. Most would agree that verses 8-9 refer to things the Antichrist will do during the Tribulation. Verse 10 is clearly related to its preceding context and speaks of something that will take place during the Tribulation.

Third, verses 11-12 further explain verses 8-10. It has been argued that when Paul said "God will send them strong delusion," his use of the future tense in the verb seems to support the notion that this is a future deluding influence. However, the future tense does not support that view. Instead, it refers to the whole of what is being said in verses 11-12. The future tense in the passage relates to the acts of unbelief (taking place during the Tribulation) as well as God's judgmental response. Verse 12 provides the purpose for God's judgment during the Tribulation, which is to judge unbelief.

The Bible teaches that all humanity is fallen and depraved (Genesis 6:5; 8:21; Jeremiah 17:10; Ephesians 4:17-18). All unbelievers, from Adam to today, are described as being spiritually dead (Ephesians 2:1-3) and blind (2 Corinthians 4:4). Thus, for any individual to believe the gospel at any time in history requires a supernatural work of the Holy Spirit to regenerate and open the sinner's eyes to God's gracious offer.

Left to ourselves, we will reject the gospel when it is preached. What sinner, who is spiritually dead and blind, has ever heard and understood the gospel without the miraculous work of God enabling him to see and believe? No sinner has ever done this on their own. No, unbelievers who are unaided by the sovereign work of God will remain in their unbelief and rejection both during the current church age as well as during the future generation. Thus, every unbeliever will have an opportunity to hear and believe the gospel during the Tribulation regardless of the extent of the evangelism he has received before the rapture.

Revelation 13:8-10 says the following in conjunction with the rise of the Antichrist at the midpoint of the Tribulation:

> All who dwell on the earth will worship him, whose names have not been written in the Book of Life of the Lamb slain from the foundation of the world. If anyone has an ear, let him hear. He who leads into captivity shall go into captivity; he who kills with the sword must be killed with the sword. Here is the patience and the faith of the saints.

Such language about belief and unbelief during the Tribulation—in relation to the Antichrist—does not support the view that some will be unable to become saved during the Tribulation. Instead, it speaks of destiny as the factor determining one's salvation: God's sovereign will! In other words, anyone who becomes saved during the Tribulation will do so in the same manner as those who become saved during the present church age—by believing the gospel and receiving Christ by faith.

Some who advocate the view that no salvation is possible in the Tribulation for those who previously heard the gospel and rejected it say that if their view is not true, then some unbelievers will be given a "second chance." This is also faulty thinking based upon a mischaracterization. The notion of a second chance, which no one will ever receive, relates to those who have departed this life through death and have gone into eternity without Christ. That is not what will happen when an unbeliever is left behind at the rapture. Instead, all unbelievers will simply be passing from one phase of history (the present church age) into another phase (the Tribulation). They are not leaving history and passing into eternity yet. All unbelievers passing from the church age into the Tribulation will continue to have an opportunity to receive Christ until they have been either saved, killed, or have received the mark of the Beast.

We can see that 2 Thessalonians 2 is a summary of Antichrist's "career" during the Tribulation period. Nothing in the text even suggests a relationship between things that will happen during the Tribulation as opposed to the church age.

What's more, we believe that millions of unbelievers will be saved during the Tribulation. For that we can all be thankful. Those who become saved will include people who had heard the gospel many times before the rapture. In the meantime, we, as believers, should make every effort to preach the gospel of God's grace so that as many people as possible will become believers and thus escape the horrors of the Tribulation.

As a side note, even though we are intensely interested in seeing as many people as possible come to Christ, the ends do not justify the means. We should not exceed the bounds of Scripture in our proclamation. Adding threats that God has not actually made will not result in a single individual being saved who would not otherwise come to faith. People are saved by the preaching of the gospel in conjunction with the power of the Holy Spirit—a power that only God can supply. At the same time, we can certainly urge people to receive Christ as Savior while they can and not take a chance on their eternal destiny. We can tell them what the Bible says: "Now is the accepted time; behold, now is the day of salvation" (2 Corinthians 6:2).

Revelation 11 speaks of two individuals called the "two witnesses." Who are they, and what is their purpose during the Tribulation?

According to Revelation 11:3-14, there will arise two unique witnesses who proclaim the gospel for a period of 1260 days during the Tribulation. Their supernatural ministry is related to Jerusalem and the nation of Israel, in which they perform a special witness to God's program of judgment.

Some speculate that the two witnesses will be Enoch and Elijah, since both were raptured alive into heaven without ever dying (Genesis 5:24; 2 Kings 2:11). They quote Hebrews 9:27, "It is appointed for men to die once, but after this the judgment," assuming both men will return and die. However, we must remember that all those who will be "caught up" alive in the rapture will not die either (1 Thessalonians 4:13-18).

Most prophecy teachers have identified the two witnesses as Moses and Elijah or two future Jewish preachers who will come in the spirit of Moses and Elijah. Reasons for such an identification include the fact that both Moses and Elijah were involved as witnesses to Christ at the transfiguration, which anticipated the second coming of Jesus (Matthew 17:3). In addition, Malachi 4:5 states that

Elijah will be sent again by God to Israel "before the coming of the great and dreadful day of the LORD." Thus, since one is clearly identified (Elijah), then it appears likely that Moses would aid Elijah in this ministry that will take place during the Tribulation.

These two individuals, specially sealed by God to serve as witnesses to Jerusalem and Israel, will arise probably during the first half of the Tribulation. Like the prophets of the Old Testament, the two witnesses will be able to perform miracles, and they will be protected by God against those who try to harm them before their mission is complete. Like Moses, they will turn water to blood, and like Elijah, they will call down fire from heaven (Revelation 10:3-6). For three-and-a-half years they will minister in Jerusalem without being harmed. At the end of the 1260 days, God will remove their special protection so that the Antichrist is able to kill them. Their bodies will be left in the streets of Jerusalem for three-and-a-half days, after which God will resurrect them and rapture them to heaven. Once they have ascended to heaven a great earthquake will occur, destroying a tenth of Jerusalem and killing 7000 people (Revelation 11:13).

The two witnesses will be clothed in sackcloth (Revelation 11:3), which is symbolic of the fact that they are prophets of doom (see Isaiah 37:1-2; Daniel 9:3). While Jerusalem is not mentioned by name as the city of their ministry, Revelation 11:7 says, "Their dead bodies will lie in the street of the great city which spiritually is called Sodom and Egypt, where also our Lord was crucified." The reference to the crucifixion clearly places these two witnesses in Jerusalem. The reference to Sodom and Egypt implies that during this time there will be licentious behavior in the city and Jewish people will be persecuted because the Antichrist will be in control.

Has most Bible prophecy already been fulfilled?

Various forms of the view called preterism teach that all, or most, Bible prophecies were fulfilled in the past in the destruction of Jerusalem in AD 70. Preterism is the view that rejects the future fulfillment of prophecies having to do with the rapture, the Tribulation, the return of Israel to the Promised Land, the rise of the future Antichrist, the Battle of Armageddon, and in some cases even the literal return of Jesus Christ.

Preterists argue that major prophetic portions of Scripture, such as the Olivet Discourse and the book of Revelation, were fulfilled in events surrounding the first-century destruction of Jerusalem by the Romans. Preterists believe that they are compelled to take such a view because Matthew 24:34 and its parallel passages say that "this generation will by no means pass away till all these things take place." They say this means the prophecies had to have been fulfilled during the first century. They believe in a local fulfillment in Jerusalem in the past, rather than a worldwide fulfillment in the future. Most preterists believe that we are currently living in at least an inaugurated new heavens and new earth on account of their view that the prophecies in the book of Revelation had to have a first-century fulfillment.

The preterist view greatly reduces the hope of the future fulfillment of hundreds of significant Bible prophecies. For example, most preterists teach that Satan is already bound by the power of the cross; therefore, they foresee no future binding of Satan as described in Revelation 20:2-3. However, those verses teach that Satan will be chained down and won't be able to get out of the abyss to deceive the nations. The very fact that worldwide deception still exists today disproves the preterists' view. Both the apostles Paul and Peter referred to the present resistance of Satan long after the cross (2 Corinthians 12:7; Ephesians 2:2; 1 Peter 5:8). Satan will not be completely bound until the millennial reign of Christ on earth.

When will the rapture take place?

The Bible makes it clear that there will be a rapture (a time when those who "sleep in Jesus" and we who are "alive and remain" will be caught up to meet the Lord in the air (1 Thessalonians 4:13-18). The big question is this: *When* will the rapture occur?

Those of us who believe that our Lord will rapture the church out of this world *before* the seven-year Tribulation are known as *pretribulationists* ("pre"= before). We believe pretribulationism provides the best answer to the question "Why the rapture?" Pretribulationism has a distinct purpose for the rapture that harmonizes with God's multifaceted plan for history.

For other viewpoints, the rapture is more of a problem that gets in the way of their overall perspectives rather than functioning as a blessed hope. These other views must awkwardly cram the rapture event into their prophetic schemes, thus finding no real purpose for that event.

For example, if the rapture and second coming occur simultaneously, as in *posttribulationism*, then it seems strange that believers would be translated to heaven (rapture) at the same time that Christ is returning to the earth (second coming) to reign for 1000 years. Such a "yo-yo" view of the rapture lacks purpose. Pretribulationism not only does not have such internal problems; rather, it thrives on its teaching that the rapture precedes the Tribulation while the second coming follows it. Notice the biblical implications of the rapture and ask yourself which view of its timing best fits with those purposes.

First Thessalonians 4:17 describes the translation of believers from their current bodies to their glorified resurrection bodies as they meet the Lord in the air. The Bible records similar meetings in the past, but the rapture of the church will be the first group meeting in history. In the past, our Lord has only taken individuals to heaven via instant transport. At the rapture, He will take a huge multitude. Are you ready?

The various rapture events of Scripture are incidents in which God takes a believer to the next life apart from experiencing the curse of death. Let's look at some of the raptures that have already taken place in the past.

As far as the biblical account goes, Enoch was the first individual to be raptured and taken up to the Lord. Genesis 5:24 describes Enoch's translation to heaven in this way: "And Enoch walked with God; and he was not, for God took him" (Genesis 5:24). What does it mean that Enoch "was not, for God took him"? It means that Enoch was translated, without dying, and went directly to be with the Lord. He was raptured, to use the language of 1 Thessalonians 4:17, or he was "taken," to use the language of John 14:3. That Enoch was raptured or translated to heaven is clear when compared with the dismal refrain "and he died" that accompanied the legacies of the other patriarchs mentioned in Genesis chapter 5.

Enoch's rapture is confirmed in Hebrews 11:5, which says, "By faith Enoch was taken away so that he should not see death, 'and he was not found, because God had taken him'; for before he was taken he had this testimony, that he pleased God." The Greek New Testament word translated "taken up" (*metetethē*) is the same one selected by those who translated the Old Testament into Greek. This word conveys the idea of being removed from one place to another. Thus, it is clear that both the Genesis passage and the three-time reference to Enoch in Hebrews teach the idea of translation to heaven.

Enoch is also mentioned in Jude 14-15, but not in connection with his translation to heaven. Jude refers to the fact that Enoch gave a prophecy about God's judgment in relation to the second coming of Christ. The fact that Enoch is said to have "prophesied" makes him a prophet. The fact we can identify Enoch as a prophet gives him a connection to the prophet Elijah, who was also raptured into heaven.

Elijah is often seen as a representative of Israel's prophets. He will make some kind of visitation during the Tribulation (Malachi 4:5), and with Moses he was one of the two witnesses from the past who appeared at Christ's transfiguration (Matthew 17:3). Like Enoch, Elijah was translated to heaven without dying. Second Kings 2 records this interesting event with an emphasis upon the mode of Elijah's transportation to heaven, saying that he was taken "into heaven by a whirlwind" (verse 1). Later, in verse 11, the whirl-wind is further described as "a chariot of fire...with horses of fire." We believe this was an appearance of the Shekinah glory of God, for Hebrews 1:7 says, "...and of the angels He says, 'Who makes His angels spirits and His ministers a flame of fire.'" God marked Elijah as a genuine prophet by identifying him with His own glory and Elijah's rapture to heaven.

There are other examples in the New Testament of rapture events. These are not passages that teach the rapture of the church, but they do serve to strengthen our understanding that the rapture involves the translation of someone from one point to another. For example, Philip was "caught...away" by the Spirit of the Lord after evangelizing to the Ethiopian eunuch and was next "found at Azotus" (Acts 8:39-40), which was several miles away.

The apostle Paul mentioned that he was "caught up [raptured] to the third heaven" and received "visions and revelations of the Lord" (2 Corinthians 12:1-4). Paul's heavenly trip reminds us of Isaiah's throne room commission (Isaiah 6:1-13). Perhaps a rapture was involved in the Isaiah incident as well. Paul, via rapture, received a commission, message, and revelation that became the foundation for the purpose of the church during this age, "which in other ages was not made known to the sons of men, as it has now been revealed by the Spirit to His holy apostles and prophets" (Ephesians 3:5).

Reminiscent of Elijah, the two witnesses in Revelation 11 will be summoned "to heaven in a cloud" (verse 12). Certainly these specially commissioned and protected messengers will serve as ambassadors for our Lord to the Jewish nation during the Tribulation. But in spite of their incredible and miraculous ministries, they will be killed by the Antichrist, then resurrected and raptured three-and-a-half days later. Their two-person rapture will testify to the greater rapture of the church, which will have already taken place before the beginning of the Tribulation. Along the same line, the "male Child" (Jesus) is said to be "caught up" (Greek, *harpazo*) or raptured "to

God and His throne" in Revelation 12:5. In this passage, the ascension of Jesus into heaven is described by the same Greek word used to speak of the rapture of the church in 1 Thessalonians 4:17.

The Bible provides us with six, possibly seven, examples of the rapture of individuals. This serves as supporting evidence for the idea that the church will be raptured as well, as 1 Thessalonians 4 teaches. Those who reject the idea of a rapture suggest that the worldwide disappearance of millions is too difficult to consider as a realistic possibility. Such is not the case if the Bible is the criterion for establishing possibilities. In fact, the Bible reveals that several raptures or trips directly to heaven have already taken place. That provides us with assurance that God can take up millions of people at one moment in time. Arguments to the contrary have no biblical support.

Why is the pretribulational view of the rapture important?

Only the pretribulational view of the rapture has a meaningful position that not only best explains a purpose for the rapture, but also requires that the church be translated before the Tribulation. Other views still must accommodate a rapture at some point—during or after the Tribulation, before or after the millennium, or at the end of time prior to eternity. But each of those views negate the key reasons for the rapture: God's plan to remove Christians from the earth during a time of global judgment, and God's use of that time to give rewards to believers and for the marriage supper of the Lamb. With the saints already in heaven, their return to earth with Christ at the second coming makes sense.

By contrast, those who hold other views on the timing of the rapture run into problems. For example, posttribulationists create an impossible situation by combining the rapture and second coming because then all believers will be translated during Christ's return, leaving no believers to be judged at the sheep and goat judgment (Matthew 25:32-46), and leaving no believers on earth who have still-untranslated bodies that are able to help populate the millennial kingdom. Keep in mind that during His 1000-year reign, Christ will rule with a "rod of iron" (Revelation 19:15). He wouldn't need to do that if all believers were taken up at the end of the Tribulation (during the second coming), for then they would all have translated, perfect bodies.

Within pretribulationism, then, the purpose of the rapture is clear. It is a needed event that removes the church from earth so that God can complete His unfinished program with Israel, at which time He will bring about her conversion and many prophesied millennial blessings. The end of the church age and the corresponding rapture of the church are needed in order to avoid a conflict of purpose for the two peoples of God—Israel and the church. Since the church age is a time in which both Jewish and Gentile believers are co-equally joined within the body of Christ (Ephesians 2:13-16), it must be ended before our Lord can return and restore national Israel (Acts 15:15-18). God's single plan for history has included multiple dimensions (Ephesians 3:8-10), with Israel serving God as His earthly people and the church as His heavenly bride.

Progress in God's divine plan for Israel has been suspended through the dispersal of His elect nation throughout the world during the "times of the Gentiles" (Luke 21:24). In the meantime, God is building His church. When it comes time for our Lord to bring about Israel's destiny of fulfilling her role as "the head and not the tail" (Deuteronomy 28:13), the church will have to be removed, since there cannot be Israelite supremacy and a co-equal relationship of Jewish and Gentile believers. The rapture of Christ's bride will end the church age and return history to a time in which God will administer His plan through His elect nation of Israel.

Thus, just as the first 69 weeks ("sevens") of Daniel 9:24-27 transpired under such an administration, so will the final week (7 years) that we know as the Tribulation period. Whereas the first 69 "sevens" (483 years) were God's timetable for Israel (from the decree to rebuild Jerusalem until the death of the Messiah), so the last "seven" (7 years) will also primarily be for Israel. Since the church was not part of the first 69 "sevens," why would we think it should be a part of the last "seven"?

After the rapture, during the Tribulation, the Lord will judge those "who dwell on the earth" (Revelation 3:10) for their rejection of Jesus. He will do this by turning the covenantal curses of Israel upon the nations as a judgment for their persecution of Israel during the Diaspora (Deuteronomy 30:7).

Further, the Tribulation will result in Israel's conversion (Ezekiel 20:37-39; Zechariah 13:8-9; Romans 11:26) and recognition that Jesus is the Messiah (Zechariah 12:10). This, in turn, will bring the blessings of the millennium upon Israel and the world. Thus, we see the necessity of the church's removal before the prosecution of God's supernatural war upon the earth. This removal we call the rapture fits the biblical pattern of God's recall of His ambassador before the beginning of conflict. God's heavenly people—the church—will be brought home, clothed, and made ready for her march down the wedding aisle at the second coming. This provides a beautiful picture that fits the details of biblical prophecy into a coherent outworking of God's historical plan. As Christ's bride, who is eagerly watching and waiting, we can only respond by saying, "The Spirit and the bride say, 'Come.' And let him who hears say, 'Come!' And let him who thirsts come. Whoever desires, let him take the water of life freely" (Revelation 22:17).

How does Revelation 3:10 teach a pretribulational rapture?

Revelation 3:10 says, "Because you have kept My command to persevere, I also will keep you from the hour of trial which shall come upon the whole world, to test those who dwell upon the earth." The Greek verb *tereo* ("keep") has the basic meaning of keeping something as it is. The preposition teaming up with *tereo* is *ek* ("out of"), which produces the composite thought "keep out." This statement promises believers that they will be kept from the hour or time of the Tribulation, which is called "the hour of trial which shall come upon the whole world, to test those who dwell on the earth." The hour of testing is said to be something that will, in the future, come upon the whole earth. This "hour of trial" will be so horrible that thankfully, God, in His mercy, will keep it short (Matthew 24:22).

It is clear that this did not happen in the days of the early church, for no one can point to a time of global testing that came upon the whole world during the first century. Revelation 3:10 describes the position and status of the church during the hour of testing, and there was no such global hour of testing during the days of the early church. It describes the results of the rapture, which is that the church will be preserved outside the hour of testing. Therefore, this passage is a strong support for pretribulationism.

What is imminence in relation to the rapture?

In the New Testament, *imminency* teaches that Christ could return and rapture His church at *any moment*, without prior signs or warning (1 Corinthians 1:7; 16:22; Philippians 3:20; 4:5; 1 Thessalonians 1:10; Titus 2:13; Hebrews 9:28: James 5:7-9; 1 Peter 1:13; Jude 21; Revelation 3:11; 22:7,12,17,20). These verses indicate that Christ could return at any moment—without warning—instructing believers to live in a continual state of anticipation in expectation of the Lord's coming.

The Oxford English Dictionary tells us that an imminent event is one which is always "hanging overhead, is constantly ready to befall or overtake one; close at hand in its incidence." Other things may happen before the imminent event, but nothing else is *required* to take place before it happens. If something else must take place before an event can happen, then that event is not imminent.

Because a person never knows exactly when an imminent event will take place, he cannot count on a certain amount of time transpiring before the imminent event happens. A person cannot legitimately say that an imminent event will happen soon, because the word *soon* implies that an event must take place within a short time. By contrast, an imminent event may take place within a short time, but it does not have to do so in order to be imminent. Only pretribulationism can give a literal meaning to such an any-moment event as the rapture.

What does the "stone [that] was cut...without hands" represent in Daniel 2?

In a vision recorded in Daniel chapter 2, King Nebuchadnezzar of Babylon saw a large stone that was cut out of a mountain without human hands. This stone struck at the feet of a statue, totally destroying it (verses 44-45). Then the stone became a huge mountain that filled the whole earth. This "stone [that] was cut...without hands" is a picture of Christ's millennial kingdom. The fact it is cut without hands signifies it is of divine origin, in contrast to the various kingdoms of man that the stone destroys.

Exodus 20:25 gives insight for the rationale as to why the entrance of Christ's kingdom is depicted as a stone cut without human hands: "If you make Me an altar of stone, you shall not build it of hewn stone; for if you use your tool on it, you have profaned it." Set within the prophetic framework, this means that during the Tribulation, Christ will judge the Antichrist's kingdom without any human agency involved. He alone will crush it and wipe it out forever, preparing the way for His millennial reign and eventually His eternal kingdom in the new heavens and new earth.

What or who are the seven mountains of Revelation 17?

Revelation 17:9-10 says, "The seven heads are seven mountains on which the woman sits. There are also seven kings. Five have fallen, one is, the other has not yet come. And when he comes, he must continue a short time." The passage tells us that the seven mountains or hills are seven heads. Then it says that the seven hills are seven kings. Thus, the seven hills refer to seven kings, not literal hills as in Rome or Jerusalem, as some people say. In a similar passage that uses the same symbolism and speaks of the same issues, Daniel 7:17,23 tells us that a king also represents a kingdom.

Thus, the seven hills or kingdoms refer to those kingdoms that have persecuted Israel down through history. When Revelation 17:10 says "five have fallen," it's referring to 1) Egypt, 2) Assyria, 3) Babylon, 4) Medo-Persia, and 5) Greece. All of those empires had fallen when John was writing the book of Revelation around AD 95. The passage then says "one is," which refers to 6) Rome, the world power at the time John was writing. Finally, the texts says "the other has not yet come," which is a reference to 7) the revived Roman Empire, over which the Beast or Antichrist will reign for "a short time" in the future.

What is the seventieth week of Daniel in Daniel 9:24-27?

According to Daniel 9:27, the Antichrist will come to power during the prophetic milestone known as the "seventieth week" and after the fulfillment of the previously prophesied "sixty-nine weeks." Daniel wrote,

> He [the Antichrist] shall confirm a covenant with many for one week; but in the middle of the week he shall bring an end to sacrifice and offering. And on the wing of abominations shall be one who makes desolate, even until the consummation, which is determined, is poured out on the desolate.

The seventieth week is a future seven-year period that is synonymous with the Tribulation. This era follows the rapture of the church and will be a time of unparalleled suffering and turmoil. The seventieth week provides the time span to which a whole host of descriptive terms in the Bible are associated, such as tribulation, great tribulation, day of the Lord, day of wrath, day of distress, day

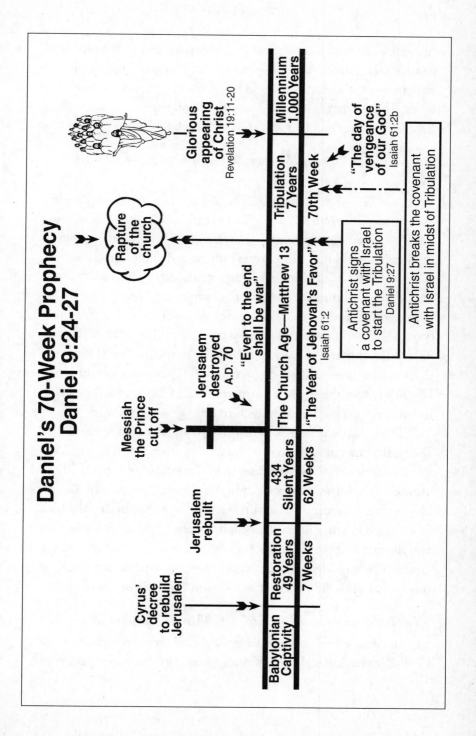

of trouble, time of Jacob's trouble, day of darkness and gloom, and wrath of the Lamb. At the beginning of the second half of the seventieth week, the Antichrist will break the covenant he made with Israel. This is what is referred to as "time and times and half a time" (Daniel 12:7; see also Daniel 7:27 and Revelation 12:14).

Where will the 200-million-man army in Revelation 9:16 come from?

As we read about what happens during the sixth trumpet judgment (Revelation 9:13-21), we find mention of an army that numbers "two hundred million" (Revelation 9:16). Many prophecy teachers contend that this army is human and comes from the East, perhaps from China. However, the text also says, "Release the four angels who are bound at the great river Euphrates" (verse 14). We are then told that these angels "were released to kill a third of mankind" (verse 15). Then we are told that it is the 200-million-man army that kill a third of mankind (verses 16-18). Thus, the passage clearly says that the four angels kill a third of mankind. The description in verses 17-19 describes the demonic army of 200 million, which explains the means used by the four angels to destroy so many.

The army is described as coming from east of the Euphrates River. Today, this area includes half of Iraq, all of Iran, Pakistan, Afghanistan, the former Soviet Islamic republics, and all of Indonesia. There are more Muslims east of the Euphrates River than west of it. Could this be one last great jihad against Israel? The text supports the idea of a demonic army because of their angelic (demonic) leadership and the fact that the description of the riders and horses are strange creatures, not modern military equipment. Whatever, and whoever, this army is, it is obvious they are demon-inspired and possessed.

What is the "little book" or "little scroll" in Revelation 10?

The "little book" in Revelation 10 clearly refers to some form of God's prophetic word to mankind. More specifically, it appears to contain Old Testament prophecies of judgment against the enemies of God and the resulting salvation for believers. Since the angel is said to put one foot on the land and the other in the sea (verse 2), it clearly indicates the prophecies in the book or scroll relate to judgments involving the land and sea. The angel is then told to give the scroll to John, which he was to eat (verse 9).

At first, John described the scroll as having a sweet taste. But later, in his stomach, it became bitter (verse 10). It appears the sweetness refers to the pleasing effect the knowledge of judgment against evil brings to God's people. And the bitterness is likely the result of realizing the bitterness of judgment when digested and thought about. The little scroll judgment teaches us that God has a plan of judgment that has already been revealed through the Old Testament prophets. This plan will be applied during the second half of the Tribulation.

Is America in Bible prophecy?

No one disputes the fact that America has a unique history during which it became, and continues to be, a preeminent military and political power in global affairs. In a quarter of a millennium, America has become a nation unlike any other nation in the history of the world. In some respects, it rivals nations with much longer histories. Yet the Bible is remarkably silent with regard to America's role in Bible prophecy. One of the hardest things for American prophecy students to accept is that the United States is not clearly mentioned in Bible prophecy, yet our nation is the preeminent superpower in the world today.

Rarely, if ever, does anyone ask, "How does Mexico, or Canada, or Chile fit into Bible prophecy?" We have to realize that some things simply are not mentioned in Scripture. What prophecy students find to be baffling is the idea that the United States is not mentioned even though it has a strong Christian heritage and is a superpower. They find it hard to envision a prophetic scenario which excludes America, the world's most influential nation.

But a review of the Bible reveals there are no specific references to the United States in Bible prophecy. The closest anyone can come is to look at biblical statements about what the nations of the world in general will be doing during the Tribulation. Passages like Haggai 2:6-7, Isaiah 66:18-20, and Zechariah 12:2-3 speak of all the nations involved in end-time events. These kinds of references might happen to include the United States in their fulfillment, but they do not teach us anything specifically about America in relation to Bible prophecy.

Some speculate that the "merchants of Tarshish" in Ezekiel 38:13 refer to the European nations and, by extension, could include America as one of the "young lions" (transplanted Europeans) who object to the invasion of Israel by Gog and Magog. However, the text of Ezekiel chapters 38–39 makes it clear that these nations do not actually come to Israel's rescue, which seems to indict America's current policy of avoiding direct support for Israel.

Others believe that America will no longer be a significant political-social-military force after the rapture. Therefore, they assume America is not mentioned because she is no longer a significant player on the world scene. Still others interpret the end-times "Babylon" as a symbolic name for America, since this "Babylon" is described as the commercial leader of the world in the last days (see Revelation 17–18).

No matter which viewpoint interpreters assume, one thing is clear: America is not specifically identified by name in end-times prophecies. What's more, the focal point of the vast majority of biblical prophecies about the latter days is Israel. That nation alone is the geographical center of God's plan for the end times.

What is the first mention of Israel in the Bible?

In Genesis 32:28, God changed Jacob's name to Israel. The passage reads: "Your name shall no longer be called Jacob, but Israel; for you have struggled with God and with men, and have prevailed." As the father of 12 sons, Jacob became the patriarch of the "sons of Israel," who in turn were the ancestors of the 12 tribes of Israel (Genesis 49:28).

Why does Israel hold a unique place in the Bible?

The prophet Isaiah wrote: "Thus says the Lord, who created you, O Jacob, and He who formed you, O Israel...I have called you by your name; you are Mine" (43:1). In Deuteronomy 7:6, Moses declared, "You are a holy people to the Lord your God; the Lord your God has chosen you to be a people for Himself, a special treasure above all the peoples on the face of the earth." God created Israel and chose them to be His people. Through them, He revealed His Word, gave His law, communicated His promises, revealed His future purposes, and ultimately sent His Messiah.

What was Jesus' relationship to Israel in the New Testament?

The New Testament begins with the genealogy of Jesus as a Jew (Matthew 1:1-17). He is a descendant of Abraham, Isaac, Jacob, Judah, and David. Jesus' claim to be the Messiah (the Christ) was linked to his lineage to the "house...of David" (Luke 2:4). As a Jew, Jesus regularly attended the synagogue (Luke 4:16). When challenged by the Samaritan woman at the well, Jesus clearly affirmed, "Salvation is of the Jews" (John 4:22). When she replied that the Messiah will come and answer everyone's questions, Jesus told her, "I who speak to you am He" (John 4:26).

Why did Jesus tell His disciples to go only to the lost sheep of Israel?

Jesus first sent the disciples to the "house of Israel" to proclaim that the kingdom of heaven was at hand. In Matthew 10:5, He told them not to go to the Gentiles or the Samaritans. Yet later He would do both (Matthew 15:21-28; Luke 10:22; John 4:4). After His resurrection, Jesus would command His disciples to take the gospel to "all the nations" (Matthew 28:19; see also Luke 24:47). As early as His preaching in the synagogue at Nazareth (Luke 4:23-27), Jesus made it clear that God was willing to bless the Gentiles (non-Jews).

So why the command to go only to the Jews? One, Jesus was reaching out first to His own people. He would later tell the disciples to be His witnesses "in Jerusalem, and in all Judea and Samaria, and to the end of the earth" (Acts 1:8). The apostle Paul also expressed the idea of taking the gospel to "the Jew first" (Romans 1:16). Two, Jesus offered the kingdom promise to the Jews in fulfillment of the Old Testament prophecies. Only after they clearly rejected His offer did He announce that He would build His church (Matthew 16:18). From that point on He was focused on going to Jerusalem to die and be raised the third day (Matthew 16:21).

Did Israel's rejection of Christ cause them to lose their covenant promises?

The apostle Paul, himself a Jew, answers this very decisively. In Romans 11:1, he asks, "Has God cast away His people? Certainly not!" Throughout Romans 9–11, Paul makes it clear that Israel's rejection was not final. There is still a "remnant" of Jewish believers (Romans 11:5), and once the fullness of the Gentiles has come, "all Israel" will be saved when the Deliverer comes (11:26). God's unconditional covenant with Abraham was the basis of all God's covenants with Israel. God promised Abraham that his descendants (his seed) would become a great nation (Israel) in the Promised Land and that through him all the nations on earth would be blessed (Genesis 12:1-3). That global blessing is realized through Abraham's descendant, Jesus the Messiah, the Savior of all people.

If believers are all one in Christ, doesn't that eliminate national distinctions in the church age?

No, not at all. While we are all brothers and sisters in God's family, our national distinctions still remain. God has a sovereign purpose for the nations of the world. Spiritual unity does not eliminate national diversity. Revelation 21:24-26 even affirms the existence of nations in the eternal state. Michael Vlach writes, "The presence of plural nations in the eternal state indicates that it is not God's purpose to make everyone Israel as non-dispensationalists often claim. There is no indication that the nations in Revelation 21 and 22 are all identified as 'Israel.' Israel's role is to bring blessings to the nations, not to make everybody Israel."[1]

Can we really equate the modern state of Israel with biblical Israel?

Absolutely! DNA evidence alone confirms that Israelis are of Jewish descent, even though many have intermarried with other nationalities. The same was true of biblical Israelites. Judah fathered sons by Tamar, a Canaanite (Genesis 38:1-30). Joseph fathered the tribes of Ephraim and Manasseh by Asenath, an Egyptian (Genesis 41:45-52). Moses fathered sons by Zipporah, a Midianite (Exodus 2:16-22). Boaz married Ruth, a Moabite, and they became ancestors of David and Jesus (Ruth 4:5-17). If all of these, and many more, were considered to be Jewish, why would modern Israelis not be considered Jewish? They certainly consider themselves to be Jewish, and so did Adolf Hitler!

Nonpremillennialists often attempt to separate modern Israel from biblical Israel by asserting that the modern state of Israel does not have a right to claim God's blessing through the Abrahamic covenant. But the Abrahamic covenant was an unconditional guarantee of the land to Abraham's descendants (Genesis 15:18-21). By contrast. The Mosaic covenant promised either blessing or cursing to the people of Israel in the land based upon their obedience or disobedience (Deuteronomy 28). While disobedience could result in their temporary expulsion from the land, God always promised to bring the people back to the land in the last days (Amos 9:11-15).

When will Israel be saved?

In Romans 11:26, the apostle Paul predicted, "All Israel will be saved." This obviously does not mean every Jew, from all time, will be saved. Nor does it mean everyone living in Israel will be saved. The prophet Zechariah predicted there is coming a time when God will pour out the Spirit of grace upon the inhabitants of Jerusalem, who will then cry out to Him whom they had pierced (12:10). But he also predicted that only one-third of the nation would turn to the Messiah during the time of Tribulation (13:8-9). Jesus predicted that He would not come again until the people of Jerusalem said, "Blessed is he who comes in the name of the Lord!" (Matthew 23:39). This will occur during the Tribulation and before Christ sets up His millennial kingdom on earth (Isaiah 62:11). At that time, the Messiah will come to rule over all the nations of the earth, including Israel. And all the saved of Israel will enter into His glorious kingdom (Isaiah 60:1-5).

Bibliography

Ankerberg, John and Dillon Burroughs. *Middle East Meltdown*. Eugene, OR: Harvest House, 2007.

———— and Jimmy DeYoung. *Israel Under Fire*. Eugene, OR: Harvest House, 2009.

Gold, Dore. *The Fight for Jerusalem: Radical Islam, the West, and the Future of the Holy City*. Washington, DC: Regnery Publishing, 2007.

Hindson, Ed. *15 Future Events That Will Shake the World*. Eugene, OR: Harvest House, 2014.

————. *Revelation: Unlocking the Future*. Chattanooga, TN: AMG Publishers, 2002.

Hitchcock, Mark. *The End*. Carol Stream, IL: Tyndale House, 2012.

Hocking, David. *Israel: Chosen by God*. Tustin, CA: HFT Publications, 2011.

Horner, Barry. *Future Israel: Why Christian Anti-Judaism Must Be Challenged*. Nashville: B&H, 2007.

Hunt, Dave. *A Cup of Trembling*. Eugene, OR: Harvest House, 1995.

Ice, Thomas and Timothy Demy. *Fast Facts on Bible Prophecy*. Eugene, OR: Harvest House, 1997.

————. *When the Trumpet Sounds.* Eugene, OR: Harvest House, 1995.

Jeremiah, David. *Agents of the Apocalypse: A Riveting Look at the Key Players of the End Times.* Carol Stream, IL: Tyndale House, 2014.

————. *What in the World Is Going On?* Nashville: Thomas Nelson, 2008.

Kay, Arthur, W. *The Rebirth of the State of Israel: Is It of God or of Men?* Grand Rapids: Baker, 1976.

LaHaye, Tim. *Revelation Unveiled.* Grand Rapids: Zondervan, 1999.

———— and Ed Hindson. *The Essential Guide to Bible Prophecy.* Eugene, OR: Harvest House, 2012.

———— and Ed Hindson. *The Popular Encyclopedia of Bible Prophecy.* Eugene, OR: Harvest House, 2004.

———— and Jerry Jenkins. *Are We Living in the Last Days?* Wheaton, IL: Tyndale House, 1999.

———— and Thomas Ice. *Charting the End Times.* Eugene, OR: Harvest House, 2001.

———— and Craid Parshall. *The Edge of Darkness.* New York: Bantam/Dell, 2006.

Larson, David. *Jews, Gentiles, and the Church.* Grand Rapids: Zondervan, 1995.

Lutzer, Erwin. *The Cross in the Shadow of the Crescent.* Eugene, OR: Harvest House, 2013.

————. *The King Is Coming.* Chicago: Moody Press, 2012.

MacArthur, John. *The Second Coming.* Wheaton, IL: Crossway Books, 1999.

———— and Richard Mayhue. *Christ's Prophetic Plans: A Futuristic Premillennial Primer.* Chicago: Moody Press, 2012.

Pentecost. J. Dwight. *Things to Come: A Study in Biblical Eschatology.* Grand Rapids: Zondervan, 1964.

Price, Randall. *Unholy War.* Eugene, OR: Harvest House, 2001.

Rydelnik, Michael. *The Messianic Hope: Is the Hebrew Bible Really Messianic?* Nashville: B&H, 2010.

Vlach, Michael J. *Has the Church Replaced Israel? A Theological Evaluation.* Nashville: B&H, 2010.

Walvoord, John. *Major Bible Prophecies.* Grand Rapids: Zondervan, 1991.

———— with Mark Hitchcock. *Armageddon, Oil, and Terror.* Carol Stream, IL: Tyndale House, 2007.

Notes

A New and Growing Crisis

1. Tim LaHaye and Thomas Ice, *Charting the End Times* (Eugene, OR: Harvest House, 2001), 84.

Chapter 1—Israel in the Crossfire

1. "Iran's Khamenei proposes plan for Israel's elimination—on Twitter." Accessed at http://www.haaretz.com/mobile/1.625465?v=AA9129CFE3E0BD9A6E8 A841B53A46B7A.

2. "Iran's Khamenei proposes plan for Israel's elimination—on Twitter," *Haaretz*, November 9, 2014.

3. "Russia Reaches Deal with Iran to Construct Nuclear Power Plants," *New York Times*, November 11, 2014. Accessed at http://www.nytimes.com/2014/11/12/ world/europe/russia-to-build-2-nuclear-plants-in-iran-and-possibly-6-more .html?_r=0. See also "Iran Nuclear Threat Greater Than Claimed," *The Sunday Times*, November 9, 2014. Accessed at http://www.thesundaytimes .co.uk/sto/news/world_news/Middle_East/article1481544.ece.

4. "Abbas: Closure of Al-Aqsa amounts to 'declaration of war,'" *Haaretz*, October 30, 2014. Accessed at http://www.haaretz.com/news/diplomacy -defense/1.623602.

5. "Five Killed in Jerusalem Synagogue Terror Attack," *Haaretz*, November 18, 2014. Accessed at http://www.haaretz.com/news/national/1.627084#!.

6. Jay Sekulow, *Rise of ISIS: A Threat We Can't Ignore* (Kindle Location 158), Howard Books Kindle Edition, 2014.

7. "Obama admits ISIS threat was misjudged as U.S. splits emerge," CNN, September 28, 2014. Accessed at http://www.cnn.com/2014/09/28/politics/obama-isis-congress/.

8. Damien McElroy, "1,803 assassinations, 4,465 car bombs: ISIS publishes detailed figures on terror campaign," *The Telegraph*, June 19, 2014. Accessed at http://news.nationalpost.com/2014/06/19/isis-laid-out-its-deadly-plans-in-annual-report-given-to-potential-donors-to-iraqi-terror-group/.

9. "Iraqi civilian death toll passes 5,500 in wake of Isis offensive," *The Guardian*, July 18, 2014. Accessed at http://www.theguardian.com/world/2014/jul/18/iraqi-civilian-death-toll-5500-2014-isis.

10. Mark Gollom, "ISIS by the numbers," CBC News, August 26, 2014. Accessed at http://www.cbc.ca/news/world/isis-by-the-numbers-how-big-strong-and-rich-the-militant-organization-may-be-1.2746332.

11. Gollom, "ISIS by the numbers," CBC News, August 26, 2014.

12. Tova Dvorin, "ISIS Destroys Tombs of Biblical Prophets Jonah, Daniel," *Israel National News*, July 27, 2014. Accessed at http://www.israelnationalnews.com/News/News.aspx/183392#!.

13. Kirsten Powers, "A Global Slaughter of Christians, but America's Churches Stay Silent," *The Daily Beast*, September 27, 2014. Accessed at http://www.thedailybeast.com/articles/2013/09/27/a-global-slaughter-of-christians-but-america-s-churches-stay-silent.html#.

14. J. Boykin, accessed at https://www.facebook.com/generalboykin/posts/395339147284592.

15. Joel C. Rosenberg, "Train wreck in U.S.-Israel relations," Joel C. Rosenberg's Blog, October 29, 2014. Accessed at https://flashtrafficblog.wordpress.com/2014/10/29/train-wreck-in-u-s-israel-relations-senior-obama-official-calls-netanyahu-vulgar-name-signalling-red-hot-hostility-between-two-governments-heres-the-latest/.

16. Jeffrey Goldberg, "The Crisis in U.S.-Israel Relations Is Officially Here," *The Atlantic*, October 28, 2014. Accessed at http://www.theatlantic.com/international/archive/2014/10/the-crisis-in-us-israel-relations-is-officially-here/382031/. See also Spencer Ho, "PM Says Personal Attacks Will Not Deter Him from Defending State," *Times of Israel*, October 29,

2014. Accessed at http://www.timesofisrael.com/pm-says-personal-attacks -will-not-deter-him-from-defending-state/.

17. Joel Rosenberg, "If Obama's Team Is Hostile to Israel Before the Elections…" Flash Traffic Blog, October 29, 2014. Accessed at https://flashtrafficblog.word press.com/2014/10/30/if-the-obama-team-is-this-hostile-to-israel-before-the -elections-how-bad-will-things-get-after-tuesday-will-the-president-turn -against-israel-appease-iran-analysis/.

18. Jay Sekulow, *Rise of ISIS: A Threat We Can't Ignore* (Kindle Locations 189-201), Howard Books Kindle Edition, 2014.

19. Ben Winsor, "Hundreds of Westerners Have Joined ISIS—Here's Where They Came From," *Business Insider,* August 27, 2014. Accessed at http://www .businessinsider.com/isis-is-recruiting-westerners-countries-2014-8.

20. "Jewish Leaders Call on European Group to Address Rising Anti-Semitism," *JSpace News*, November 13, 2014. Accessed at http://www.jspacenews.com/ jewish-leaders-call-european-group-address-rising-anti-semitism/.

21. Suzanne Fields, "The Israelization of anti-Semitism," *The Washington Times*, September 14, 2014. Accessed at http://www.washingtontimes.com/ news/2014/sep/17/fields-the-israelization-of-anti-semitism/.

22. Cathy Young, "Europe's Problem with Growing Anti-Semitism," Reason .com, November 18, 2014. Accessed at http://reason.com/archives/2013/11/18/ europes-problem-with-growing-anti-semiti.

23. Adam Lebor, "Exodus: Why Europe's Jews Are Fleeing Once Again," *Newsweek*, July 29, 2014. Accessed at http://www.newsweek.com/2014/08/08/ exodus-why-europes-jews-are-fleeing-once-again-261854.html.

Chapter 2—The Beliefs of Israel's Enemies

1. Don Belt, ed., *The World of Islam* (Washington, DC: National Geographic 2001), 128-75. See also J. Ankerberg and J. Weldon, *Fast Facts on Islam* (Eugene, OR: Harvest House, 2001), 13-18.

2. "10,000 Extremist Websites on the Internet," *Emirates 24/7*, March 26, 2013. Accessed at http://www.webcitation.org/query?url=http://www.emir ates247.com/news/region/10-000-extremist-websites-on-internet-expert -2013-03-26-1.500188&date=2013-03-27.

3. Kevin Sullivan, "Three American Teens, Recruit Online, Caught Trying to Join the Islamic State," *Washington Post*, December 8, 2014. Accessed at http://www.washingtonpost.com/world/national-security/three-american

-teens-recruited-online-are-caught-trying-to-join-the-islamic-state/2014/
12/08/8022e6c4-7afb-11e4-84d4-7c896b90abdc_story.html.

4. Gregory M. Davis, "Islam 101," JihadWatch.org. Accessed at http://www
.jihadwatch.org/islam-101.

5. See at http://www.fordham.edu/halsall/source/pact-umar.html.

6. See at http://www.apinfo.eu/fatimapoem.pdf.

7. Robert Evans, "Atheists face death in 13 countries, global discrimination:
study," Reuters, December 9, 2013. Accessed at http://www.reuters.com/
article/2013/12/10/us-religion-atheists-idUSBRE9B900G20131210.

8. Kersten Knipp, "Saudi Religious Police Crack Down on Bloggers,"
DW.de, December 5, 2014. Accessed at http://www.dw.de/saudi-religious
-police-crack-down-on-bloggers/a-18113104.

9. Lucinda Borkett-Jones, "Iraqi churches used as Islamic State prisons," Chris
tiantoday.com, December 4, 2014. Accessed at http://www.christiantoday
.com/article/iraqi.churches.used. as.islamic.state.prisons/43866.htm.

10. "More than 1200 Iraqis killed in November by acts of terrorism and violence," Fox News, December 1, 2014. Accessed at http://www.foxnews.com/
world/2014/12/01/more-than-1200-iraqis-killed-in-november-by-acts-terror
ism-and-violence/.

11. These figures can be accessed at http://www.thereligionofpeace.com/. There
is a running list that goes back to 9/11, and each month's figures are summa-
rized in the left column on the home page.

Chapter 3—The Miracle of Israel's Existence

1. The text of the Balfour Declaration accessed at http://www.jewishvirtual
library.org/jsource/History/baltoc.html.

Chapter 5—Answering the Three Key Questions

1. *The New Defenders Study Bible* (Nashville: Thomas Nelson, 2006), 1438 (Matthew 24:6).

Chapter 7—Israel as a Fig Tree

1. David L. Cooper, "Rules of Interpretation," *Biblical Research Monthly,* 1947,
1949. Accessed at http://www.biblicalresearch.info/page7.html.

Chapter 8—The Miracle of Israel's Regathering

1. Rabbi Menachem Kohen, *Prophecies for the Era of Muslim Terror* (Brooklyn, NY: Lamda Publishers, 2000), 26.

2. James Combs, "Israel in Two Centuries," in the *Tim LaHaye Prophecy Study Bible* (Chattanooga, TN: AMG Publishers, 2000), 874.

3. Combs, "Israel in Two Centuries," 874.

Chapter 9—The Growing Russian-Islamic Threat

1. Mark Hitchcock, "Gog and Magog," in the *Tim LaHaye Prophecy Study Bible* (Chattanooga, TN: AMG Publishers, 2000), 876.

Chapter 11—The Future Millennial Kingdom

1. John Walvoord, *The Revelation of Jesus Christ* (Chicago: Moody, 1989), 325.

Appendix 2—Frequently Asked Questions

1. Michael Vlach, "What About Israel?" in *Christ's Prophetic Plans*, John MacArthur and Richard Mayhue, eds. (Chicago: Moody, 2012), 107.

Acknowledgments

With special thanks to
Dillon Burroughs
and
Michael W. Herbert,
editorial assistants

Other Books on Bible Prophecy from Harvest House Publishers

Charting the End Times

Tim LaHaye and Thomas Ice

The result of decades of research and Bible study, this landmark resource provides a fascinating picture of the end times. Includes a visual foldout, 50 color charts/diagrams, explanatory text, and clear answers to tough questions.

Charting the End Times Prophecy Study Guide

Tim LaHaye and Thomas Ice

This stand-alone study guide for individuals or groups takes readers through the high points of Bible prophecy with helpful charts that offer a clear picture of what will happen and when in the last days.

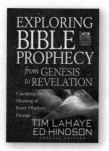

Exploring Bible Prophecy from Genesis to Revelation

Tim LaHaye and Thomas Ice, general editors

It's all here—clear and concise explanations for key prophetic passages from the beginning to the end of the Bible. Written by Bible scholars but created for lay-level Bible students, this includes useful charts, diagrams, and time lines that enhance one's understanding of Bible prophecy.

The Popular Encyclopedia of Bible Prophecy

Tim LaHaye and Ed Hindson, general editors

An A-to-Z encyclopedia filled with over 400 pages of facts, information, and charts about the last days.

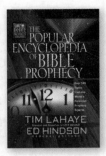

15 Future Events That Will Shake the World
Ed Hindson

As the end of the age draws near, the signs of the times will be impossible to ignore—millions of people reported missing, a new world superpower that eclipses the United States, and the Middle East crisis will appear to be resolved. How will these events affect our world? Discover God's plan for the end of this age and the beginning of the age to come.

About the Authors

Tim LaHaye, who conceived the all-time bestselling Left Behind® series, is a renowned prophecy scholar, minister, and educator. He is the author or coauthor of more than 80 books, including *Understanding Bible Prophecy for Yourself* and *Charting the End Times*. He and his wife, Beverly, live in Southern California.

Ed Hindson is the dean and distinguished professor of religion at Liberty University in Lynchburg, Virginia. He also serves as the speaker on *The King Is Coming* telecast and has written, cowritten, or served as general editor for numerous books, including *Exploring Bible Prophecy from Genesis to Revelation*, *The Popular Handbook on the Rapture* (both with Tim LaHaye), *15 Future Events That Will Shake the World*, and *The Popular Encyclopedia of Church History*. He holds a DMin from Westminster Theological Seminary and a PhD from the University of South Africa.

To learn more about Harvest House books and
to read sample chapters, visit our website:

www.harvesthousepublishers.com

HARVEST HOUSE PUBLISHERS
EUGENE, OREGON